THE STORY OF JOSEPH
HOW GOD WORKS
IN OUR LIVES

James R. M. Young

Burning Heart Press

ISBN-13: 9781234567890
ISBN-10: 1477123456

Cover design by: Art Painter
Library of Congress Control Number: 2018675309
Printed in the United States of America

To my daughters: Dowler, Byerly, Gaelyn and Shelby

And, to Anne

When a man believes in God's providence, he does not know only in abstracto and generally that God is over all things and all things are in his hand, but he continually sees something of the work of this hand, and may continually see God's will and purpose in very definite events, relationships, connextions and changes in the history of created being.

KARL BARTH, CHURCH DOGMATICS, III/3, P. 23

CONTENTS

INTRODUCTION

There is a tendency today among younger adults and teenagers to think that Bible stories are close to fairy tales: they're about strange events, with things sometimes happening that are not ordinary. Yet they are supposed to have some sort of 'moral' you take away from reading them, like, don't steal, don't lie, be a good boy, be a good girl.

I'm afraid that, as a minister and especially as a Christian educator who has worked with children a lot, I and a whole lot of people like me, have to take responsibility for such a mistaken perception of the great stories in the Bible. You see, when we would write Sunday School books and pamphlets for volunteers to use as their Sunday School lessons (not to mention the stuff written for use with teens during Sunday evening or mid-week youth group meetings), the adult-themed stuff would be omitted. Like David sleeping with Bathsheba when she was married to another man. And definitely never mention the awful truth that David, the king, ordered Bathsheba's husband, who was in the army, to the front lines so that when the army attacked the enemy he'd be killed, and then David could have Bathsheba free and clear.

No, when writing for little ones and younger teens, such things were never mentioned (which is why all you hear about David in most Sunday school curriculum is that he killed Goliath with a sling-shot and played the harp and wrote the Psalms and then he became king, leaving the implication that if YOU are a good boy or a good girl, and come to church and do what you're told, you will be a success too!) because most Sunday School teachers simply wanted some little 'moral lesson' the boys and girls could learn in forty or so minutes, with no messy complications to the story.

Having raised four daughters, I completely understand the intent, and to a large extent I agree with it.

But there's a problem with this, namely, that for most people, the Bible stories they are familiar with are the ones they learned when they were small or as young teens. This means that these stories we THINK we know, because we learned them in Sunday school, in summer Vacation Bible School, these stories were not the stories as the bible actually had them; rather, they were very sanitized versions of so many of the Bible stories.

When we adults then actually read the stories in the Bible there is often raised eyebrows, frowns, and mutterings of "I didn't realize this was in the Bible."

This is often true of the Joseph stories from Genesis. Joseph was the great-grandson of Abraham, the first of the Patriarchs, from whom the Jews (and Moslems) trace their origin. Joseph's father was Jacob, the son of Isaac, who was Abraham's son that he had when Abraham was one hundred years old. Yes, you read that right. One hundred years old!

These old stories about the Patriarchs were told and retold and then eventually written down not as cute, simple moral lessons so the Jews could be reminded how to be good boys and good girls for God. No, they were written down because God Himself interacted with these people and called them out from all other people to be his own, special ones. Everything that God said and did with these Patriarchs, along with the stories associated with them are important because they illustrate how God blesses and works with human beings. They also illustrate how ornery and mean and even despicable some people can be. Make no mistake: the Bible pulls no punches in these stories.

The thing I marvel at is how people continue to be people, good and bad, over and over, centuries ago, just like they are today. This being the case, then how God worked in these people's lives and how they responded to what was happening to them just might give us some clues about how to live for God in our very complex culture today.

So, prepare, perhaps, to be shocked by some things I'm going to share with you; but I also challenge you to open yourself to perceive the Holy Spirit at work in this story of Joseph. Then, with this Joseph story as something of a template on the mysterious workings of God, open your mind to perceive how God just might be working in your life today.

This is not just a story about how God helped

a young man going through a horrible time (it is at least that), and how this young man finally grows up and becomes a responsible, caring human being; it is also a springboard to prompt us to open our eyes to God's working today, in our personal lives, in the church we attend, perhaps even to consider how God is working beyond our churches in ways we had not considered. God is not some strange being or force far removed and a long time ago in a land far, far away; God is ALIVE, and we know this to be true because Jesus Christ is alive and with us, working with us, working in us, all around us, all the time.

BUT! There's always a but, isn't there? The 'but' in this case does not negate everything I've said so far. This 'but' leads to a deep, spiritual truth, namely that very often, we are not able to perceive God working in our lives in the present, difficult experience we're going through. We will be able to perceive this, sometimes in vague ways, sometimes with more direct ways, later. It's almost as if things are too confusing, too chaotic, too heart-breaking for us to perceive anything but the pain.

That's why it's so important to recognize that first and foremost, this story about Joseph tells us that God was with Joseph in everything that he experienced. That is the chief lesson in chapter one, and it carries through all the other chapters. The other chapters then begin presenting what really amounts to a jig-saw puzzle with each chapter functioning much like several pieces of a jig-saw puzzle. For instance, we may read a chapter and respond by thinking that this chapter, i.e., this jig-saw piece, is odd or seems to indicate that God is nowhere to be found.

It really isn't until we get to the final two chapters that the whole picture starts to make sense, and we begin to perceive how God was active in the previous parts of the story when we thought God was way off somewhere else. Although it's not a mystery where all the dots are connected in the final chapter and the 'murderer' is finally revealed, nevertheless there is very much a feeling of finally connecting the dots to reveal a picture that finally makes sense of how God just might be working not only in Joseph's life, but also our lives.

First and foremost, though, this story is the story of a family. A blended family that was amazingly dysfunctional. Perhaps not abusive as we would define the term, but definitely dysfunctional. Crazily enough, the story finally leads to a profound reconciliation among members of this family, a reconciliation that is both surprising and touching.

There is no way I can improve the terse, matter-of-fact style of the biblical narrator of this story as it is found in Genesis, chapters 37 through 47. Over the years I have come to have a deep respect for the biblical text AS IT IS, meaning first and foremost what the Hebrew or the Greek text is (The Old Testament is written in Hebrew, the New Testament is written in Greek) and how an accurate translation puts this. Then and only then asking questions, wondering about such things as what was going on behind the scenes of the text and what implications are aroused by the text.

So, I'm letting the text speak for itself and then presenting what I believe are responses to implications and questions arising from the text. I am utilizing the most accurate translation I'm familiar with, the New Revised Standard Version. These are the sections of the chapters printed in bold. Occasionally I'll disagree with it, but only occasionally. Remember, the New Revised Standard is, as was its predecessor (the Revised Standard Version) the product of a fairly large committee. Certainly, this committee consisted of leading scholars in the field of Biblical languages and particularly scholars known for their scholarly work in the individual books of the Bible. This is all very good. Nevertheless, it's still a committee. And committees are always governed by a majority vote. We almost never hear what the minority thought. I like to think of myself as, every now and then, giving a minority report, a slightly different translation (but still the same Hebrew or Greek) of a word or phrase within the text that, in my ever-so-humble opinion, makes better reading.

Finally, something of a personal note. It's a fair question to ask a writing minister or scholar why he was drawn to the particular texts he's writing about. For me it's because of what happened to me when I was a teenager. When I was sixteen years old, I lost my father. He had been battling for years a stomach ulcer and finally the only thing left in what treatment was available was a complex and difficult surgery that removed the ulcer along with three-quarters of his stomach. It was a hard decision to have such a surgery, but my father felt he had no other choice. He survived the initial surgery but spent the next month in the Intensive Care Unit. My mother, devoted to him as she was, left the hospital only one time for a twenty-four break. For an entire month she stayed as close to him as she could get, usually in the waiting area and then going in for a fifteen-to-twenty-minute visit every two to three hours.

Finally, after a month of going from one complication to another, my father passed away in the early morning hours of November 29, 1969, my mother and I at his bedside there in the hospital. He was just fifty-five years old.

I was devastated, as was my mother. I am an only child, and my parents had me after being married for several years. To say we three were close is putting it mildly. Now, what we had, what was the center, the core of my universe, was shattered.

It was only through the grace of my mother's love and the love of some very close friends, and the grace of God Himself that I did not, literally, go off the deep end and get into drugs, alcohol, or God knows what. But it was, though, several years before I began to really deal with my grief in any effective way, and thus discovering just how angry I was at God for taking my dad. Up to then I had seen myself as a calm, even-tempered young man who never got angry.

Yeah, right!

Of course, I got angry, just like every human being that has existed on this earth. I knew this, but what I came to perceive is that I would always tamp down deep inside every angry impulse. Push it way down deep! Because if I didn't, subconsciously I was afraid that I'd explode in anger, and this would be (at least so I thought on some deep level) absolutely disastrous. So disastrous that there would be nothing left of me. I would be destroyed.

Now, I would never have put what I was feeling way down deep into such words, but the unconscious mechanisms functioning in me were definitely geared in such a way as I felt my very existence was threatened by such anger.

Who thinks this way? Not mature adults, but children. Especially prone to this are us only children who have learned to behave in ways so as to receive praise from the gods in our lives, that is, our parents and grandparents. What most threatens us only kids? When our parents get angry at us, that's what. That's when we almost literally feel the earth slipping out from beneath our feet and we begin sliding into some deep, dark pit. To experience the anger of the gods in our lives is absolutely terrifying. So, we learn early on to tamp down deep any urge to get angry at our parents (or, for that matter, anyone else) because to do so invites terrible disaster.

When my father died, I had long learned to stifle and tamp down any angry impulses I had, especially those dealing with my dad or mom or, in fact, any authority figure. I had felt called to become a minister quite early in my life and, although I considered going into preparation for other professions, most particularly as an attorney and going to law school, I still allowed this childhood sense to continue in my thinking. Finally, I gave in to this sense of call that had, by my sophomore year in college, become overwhelming in my consciousness, and proceeded to apply to and then entered seminary.

Now, intellectually I always liked asking questions about God and the Bible and struggling mightily about such things with fundamentalist friends in junior high and high school. But to really doubt the goodness of God, to really, very, very seriously get angry with God, to actually become enraged at God for what had happened in my life, this was forbidden territory in my inner life.

But due to some prodding and poking by my supervisor and the members of my chaplaincy group, along with some things happening at the hospital where I was a student chaplain (in Clinical Pastoral Education, i.e. CPE), the psychic barriers I had erected against such feelings were chipped away and a flood of emotions connected with my father's death came rushing out.

It was the beginning of my real healing from the grief of losing my father.

It is thus from my own experience that I learned first-hand how anger, real, powerful, deep anger is always connected to serious grief. It is from my own experience that I have learned that stifling such anger leads to things that sabotage us, such as giving inappropriate outbursts of anger at inappropriate times, of self-sabotaging good relationships, at mis-perceiving things in relationships, saying that people are feeling one way when, as a matter of fact, they are not. Stifled anger also inflicts on us various bodily troubles, such as upset stomach, pain in the lower back, muscle spasms and pain in our ankles and feet.

I have experienced all of this. But, with learning to deal with my grief about my dad, I have learned to accept the simple truth that I do get angry and that I have a temper. I have also learned that it's okay, it's VERY MUCH okay, to become angry with God.

Not very many years after I was ordained, I began to study and preach on these old Joseph stories. I was amazed at what was in them, at how much in them reflected my own frustrations about life and my own dealings with my deep grief at losing my father as well as the family dynamics I had experienced when I married a girl who had three brothers! How amazingly contemporary were these old stories, and how deeply they spoke to my soul.

My first wrestlings with these texts and the sermons that emerged were received well by the small congregation I was serving. Over the years since these initial explorations, I have revisited them in nearly every congregation I've served, not simply repeating the sermons but going back and analyzing the texts again and again and again, reading the commentaries and putting new scholarly writings into dialogues in my mind with older works. Always when revisiting these stories, I learned new things and the Holy Spirit helped me to see new, different aspects of the text and implications that had never occurred to me before. When I was twenty-eight years old, I read these texts and heard the Holy Spirit speaking through them and when I'm sixty-seven I hear those things I had previously heard, but I'm also hearing other things and thinking about different implications that would never occur to my twenty-eight-year-old self.

Here then, are my (at least, as of the date of this book) mature reflections on these texts that have spoken to me so much about experiencing and coping with dark things that happen to us in life and how families work and do what they do

Even when I was twenty-eight, and the years since have only convinced me further, I had learned and continue to believe with every once of my being, that we can shoulder life, with all its burdens and tragedies, only if we have some sense of hope. Hope, real, lasting hope, comes, finally, from Jesus Christ. Through the tragedy of the cross we are helped to begin to perceive the hope of some sort of resurrection both within and beyond life. In some mysterious way, by admitting the hard but real truth that we're hurt, that we're angry, even enraged, that we don't understand why things have happened to us, admit this and not dodge it out of some misplaced sense of piety, honestly admit it, then give this to God in prayer, trusting that Jesus is still with us, that he will give us strength to keep on going and that somehow, some way, perhaps even beyond this earth, we will come to understand something of what has happened to us. This is when we Christians begin to experience little, tiny bits of hope that keep us going.

That's why I, in every one of the chapters that follow, have connected what was going on with Joseph to Jesus in some fashion. It's not that Joseph poses questions about what was happening to him that Jesus then answers, but rather that what was happening to Joseph bares some semblance to what was happening in Jesus' life or prompts Jesus' own words to embrace what happens. And, as always, everything said by and about Jesus in the New Testament is to be perceived through what happened to Jesus, that is, his death and resurrection.

Several early church Fathers, along with Luther and Calvin, said that Joseph is something of a forerunner of Christ. I agree with them. But I think Joseph is even more. I think that how God deals with Joseph, with the way Joseph's life unfolded, is something of a small window into the inner workings of God. These inner workings were finally revealed in Jesus, in his life, his words, what happened to him.

Coming at these old Joseph stories with this in mind enables us to perceive not just how God works in Joseph's life, but how God is working in our lives as well. If we're willing to let ourselves see this. This is a big 'if'.

But I hope you do.

THE STORY OF
JOSEPH

How God Works in Our Lives

CHAPTER ONE

Jacob settled in the land where his father had lived as an alien, the land of Canaan. This is the story of the family of Jacob.

Joseph, being seventeen years old, was shepherding the flock with his brothers; he was a helper to the sons of Bilhah and Zilpah, his father's wives; and Joseph brought a bad report of his brothers to their father. Now Jacob loved Joseph more than any other of his children because he was the son of his old age; and he had made him a long robe with sleeves. But when his brothers saw that their father loved him more than all his brothers, they hated him and could not speak peaceably to him. Genesis 37:1-4

What kind of young man is Joseph? A spoiled brat, that's what.

He tattles on his brothers, tells his dad what they're doing wrong, and you KNOW that he's been doing this nearly his whole life!

This endears him to his dad, Jacob, but definitely not to his brothers. And this has been going on a long time...

Now, let me point out something about the special robe Jacob purchased for Joseph. The old King James Version translated this phrase from the Hebrew as "coat of many colors". And I remember a little Sunday school book telling the story of Joseph (about the size of a thank-you note) with a little boy, about six or seven, wearing a rainbow-colored robe.

Generations of Sunday School children grew up with this image of a small boy wearing a rainbow-colored robe. And for the life of me, I could never figure out why such a garment really set the older brothers off. Because they didn't one like Joseph's, is the reason I remember being given when I asked.

"Coat of many colors' is a mistranslation of the Hebrew text, which actually means 'long-sleeves'. Instead of a 'coat of many colors' the correct translation is 'long-sleeved coat'. This mistranslation was corrected in the Revised Standard Version (1952), and 'long-sleeved' has been used in all the major translations since. Which is all well and good, but to us in our day, totally meaningless. Coat of many colors? Long-sleeved? What in the world difference does either make? Makes no sense to us, save that explanation I heard long ago in Sunday School: the other brothers didn't get such a nice, expensive coat and they were jealous.

Okay, all of us can understand that. We've been in the brothers' shoes (so to speak) sometimes, and maybe, for some of us, been in Joseph's and had to deal with sibling jealousy.

But jealous enough to want to kill their

brother?

Let me say this again: KILL THEIR BROTHER!!!!!?????

How in the world could a simple, if expensive, coat prompt such a reaction from his brothers? It makes no sense!

(and if you've known the 'Joseph and his Brothers story' for years but never thought about these things, then you're like most of us who grew up going to Sunday School and church, just accepting as true what the Bible said and what the Sunday School teachers and the Preacher(s) said and asking no questions. Hey, when we were younger it was a whole lot easier on us if we didn't make waves. Right?)

It makes no sense to us because we're unfamiliar with the culture of Joseph's Day. In that culture, people who worked for a living (so to speak), shepherds, farmers, etc. wore short tunics with no sleeves. Sleeves, especially long, billowy sleeves, get in the way when you're moving through a sheep herd, or separating them or feeding them.

Only people who did not do such manual labor wore outer garments with long sleeves. Usually this was royalty or somebody who was rich. If you had money, if you came from money, you didn't have to work with your hands, your feet and your back. You paid other people to do this for you.

And, as is always the case, such people tended to think of themselves as just a wee bit better than the laborers they hired. Most of the time they were better educated so people who had money usually spoke better, using proper words and phrases. They definitely dressed way better too, because they could afford better clothes, and so looked better than the laborers they hired. Especially in their long-sleeved garments.

Now Daddy Jacob is a fairly well-off farmer, a raiser of sheep. But he is definitely not extremely wealthy and definitely not an aristocrat or royalty. But here he goes and buys a long-sleeved coat his son, a garment only an aristocrat's offspring would wear. And notice: Jacob does this ONLY for Joseph. ONLY JOSEPH!

How many ways can we spell clueless?

By giving Joseph this coat only to Joseph, Jacob is saying to his 17-year-old son, "Joseph, you're not ever going to have work like your brothers. You're better than they are. I know it. You know it. Now, they know it too!"

Now we can comprehend the reaction of Joseph's brothers to his long-sleeved coat. The favoritism had been going on for years, but this, this coat? It was the straw that broke the camel's back. The brothers had finally had their fill of their father's ignoring all of them and focusing all his attention (and love) on Joseph. The bible is quite succinct: **"So when they saw that their father loved Joseph more than all the other brothers, they hated Joseph."**

The Bible could have proceeded from here into what the brothers did to Joseph, but the biblical narrator wants us to know a little bit more about Joseph and his relationship to his brothers and to his father. So, we now read about two early dreams Joseph had, which are a definite 'heads up' to readers because Joseph, in captivity in Egypt, makes his way out through his God-given ability to interpret dreams. It's the Bible's way of saying 'pay attention whenever dreams are mentioned in this story.'

Once, Joseph had a dream, and when he told it to his brothers, they hated him even more. He said to them, "Listen to this dream that I dreamed. There we were binding sheaves in the field. Suddenly my sheaf rose and stood upright; then your sheaves gathered around it and bowed down to my sheaf." His brothers said to him, "Are you indeed to reign over us? Are you indeed to have dominion over us?" So, they hated him even more because of his dreams and his words.

He had another dream, and told it to his brothers, saying, "Look, I have had another dream: the sun, the moon and eleven stars were bowing down to me." But when he told it to his father and to his brothers, his father rebuked him, and said to him, "what kind of dream is this that you have had? Shall we indeed

come, I and your mother and your brothers, and bow to the ground before you?" So, his brothers were jealous of him, but his father kept the matter in mind." Genesis 37:5-11

When I first read this carefully, some years ago, I remember thinking, "Joseph!!! Are you crazy? Don't you know how your brothers are going to react?" And then it hit me: of course he did. That's why he told them the dream in the first place.

The brothers knew that they could do nothing as long as Jacob was around. If they tried anything they'd all be in serious trouble.

Now, there's an interesting thing to be observed about Jacob at this point. He tells Joseph to stop talking nonsense, which is a sound thing to tell the young man. But notice, he does absolutely nothing about all his other sons hating Joseph. Nothing. He doesn't even counter the dreams, really. Just says quit talking.

In other words, Jacob is a passive father. He does not want to talk about the incredibly tense situation all around him. In fact, he pulls away from it by telling Joseph to hush.

Which is more typical of us guys than any of us want to admit. How often have you had or heard of this type of conversation:

"Honey, I'm glad you're home!!!!! Finally!!! The kids have been fighting for the last two hours, and I"

(Interrupting) "Well, deal with it. Put 'em in time out or whatever."

"Well, I've tried, but it doesn't seem to work."

"Well, ... I. ... "

"You need to talk to them."

"Uh. ...ok.. I'll. ...uh. ...I'll ... "

(Interrupting) "You need to get them to quit fighting!"

"Ok. .. ok. .. I'll, . .. I'll tell them to behave. .. "

Oh, yes, like that's going to help. . .

But you see, we guys tend to think that she's been with them more than I have, even if she does work and women are better at handling children than guys. But then we don't stop there, oh no; we go on and think that she doesn't have as much stuff to bring home as I do, and my job is a lot more stressful. . . (tell that to a teacher and see what reaction you get).

Bottom line is we dads simply don't want to deal with this sort of thing right when we walk in from work. It never seems to occur to us that our wife had just got home as well, picking up the kids and listening to them fuss all the way home in the car, and after HER day at work, the last thing she wanted to deal with was fussing children.

If you're in my generation (baby-boomer), we're also thinking things like "If I acted like my dad did when I fussed, a few whacks from the belt, some well-chosen words, and that'd be it. . . but not today. . . no sir. . . not today. . . nope, gotta TALK to 'em. . . and I'm not very good at talking to kids, especially my kids. . ."

Let's get something straight, early in this whole story arc. We know that being a dad means being present to your kids. Obviously physically present; but also being willing to notice them and not zone out, like watching a game, or tv show or movie or using the work from the office as an excuse to escape dealing with the kids. Yeah, we're awkward at talking with them and we feel real insecure doing it, but just remember we were awkward as all get out when we were first learning to ride a bicycle. But we learned, didn't we? And so it is in 'being present' to our children.

We need to learn to let the game go for a little while so that we can listen to what they're trying to tell us. We need to reschedule some meetings so we can be present at a school special event that they're involved in.

I'm fascinated that this story begins in Joseph's late teen years.

Permit me to go off on a brief tangent. Remember that little Sunday School book I mentioned earlier, the one with the picture of the little boy wearing a coat of many colors? I didn't say anything about this then, but I call your attention to what I think is even MORE troubling than the picture of the coat. Namely, that Joseph is pictured as a child. A child somewhere between six or seven years old. This is really astonishing to me, because the biblical text, even in the King James Version, says plainly that Joseph was 17 years old. He was a teenager, an older teenager, not a kid in second or third grade.

Apparently that little book (and others like it) really made the rounds of Sunday Schools back in the fifties and early sixties because not too long ago I was discussing this story of Joseph with a friend who was my age and from my hometown. She had, like I and most other kids back then, attended church with the same frequency as I did, namely Sunday School and worship on Sunday morning, Junior Choir (later Youth Group) on Sunday evening (starting anywhere from 5 to 6 PM) followed by Sunday evening worship at 7:30, with the mid-week gathering called Prayer Meeting, on Wednesdays at 7 PM, a shorter worship service, including a sermon along with prayers that lasted about forty to forty-five minutes, followed by Adult Choir, which lasted until around 9:15. My friend grew up in a Baptist church, I in a Presbyterian, but we both had almost exactly the same schedule for church. We had not seen each other in several years and at one point she inquired about what I was working on, and I told her about this project, and went on to talk about how much Joseph was a spoiled brat. On hearing this she expressed real surprise. Joseph? A Spoiled Brat? You're kidding! I shook my head and began to explain why I thought this, but she interrupted me saying, "No, NO! He was too young to be called a spoiled brat. His brothers were just jealous of him, because he was good and kind and did what his parents told him to."

I stared at my friend for a few seconds and asked her, "How old was Joseph when his father gave him that coat?" Without any hesitation she replied, "He was about six or seven." When I quietly told her the Bible said he was 17, she didn't believe me. Oh, she was polite, but I knew that she thought I was off on some wild tangent (I have no idea where she got that idea about me. . .), and would later go home, pull out her Bible and check this.

And that's precisely what she did. She texted me the next day that I was right, and she was astonished at not realizing this because there it was, "in black and white," as she wrote.

When I asked her (during the conversation the previous evening) if she remember reading the book I described, she frowned and said maybe. Well, if she didn't, then her Sunday School teacher (or her parents) definitely did, because only in Sunday School material from the fifties and early sixties have I ever seen Joseph as a child of early elementary school age, and the ETERNAL Sunday School lesson that was ALWAYS taught, E*V*E*R*Y Sunday, in some way or another, was "OBEY YOUR PARENTS! OBEY YOUR TEACHERS! BE A GOOD GIRL, BE A GOOD BOY, AND DON'T CAUSE TROUBLE!"   With this as the ultimate goal of the lesson, Joseph becomes an example of obeying Daddy Jacob, doing what Daddy Jacot wanted, being a GOOD LITTLE BOY. His mean, mean, MEAN older brothers were just jealous, and didn't want to do what Daddy Jacob said to do (being the juvenal delinquents that they were), so Joseph, by being good, made them look bad. So obviously they wanted him out of their way.

For some strange reason, it never occurred to any Sunday School teacher or parent who taught the Joseph story with this interpretation to think about how extreme a reaction it was for the brothers to want to kill their brother, and then, when they let him live, to sell their own brother into slavery. What would make his own brothers hate him so much that they did this? What had Joseph done to them? These questions never were asked.

The moral of all this: never, EVER, underestimate the power of Sunday School illustrations and pictures to shape how thousands and thousands of people have interpreted scripture over the years.

And when the young, grad school/seminary-educated preacher says something about the biblical text that goes against 'what was traditionally taught', well, a whole lot of people think, "Why, the preacher's just showin' off her/his education; it doesn't mean a thing, not really. Just nod, act polite, and then ignore it."

It's the wise preacher who, knowing what he's learned about a text and realizes it goes against what has been traditionally taught (FOR YEARS AND YEARS!!!!!) then tests this with a mix of older and younger folk BEFORE preaching it, gently inquiring about any 'old' Sunday School' pictures that go with what she or he is preaching on. Just sayin'.

Back to the text. When a family goes for years ignoring the real problems that have been going on for a long time, or focuses blame time after time on one person, things eventually come to an explosive point. Very often this is the late teen years.

This blended family (for Jacob had been married several times by the time the story begins, and he had kids from all his wives) had been smoldering for years. Joseph was never disciplined like the other boys. In fact, Joseph was allowed to do essentially whatever he wanted to do. Jacob's absolute refusal to intervene with his sons in any way, even when they talked openly of his favoritism, expressed real frustration with what was going on, over and over, for years!!!!! Jacob did nothing to deal with any of this. He continued to be passive, he continued to favor Joseph. (The obvious question is 'why?', and I have some suggestions that have to do with how he came to marry first Leah, then Rachel, along with having children by some others (yes, he did!), but that takes us outside this particular story).

The coat Jacob gave to Joseph, and gave nothing to any of the other brothers, becomes the final straw.

In family counseling there is a term, 'identified patient.' It refers to the family member that everybody says is the problem. This person might even firmly believe that he/she IS the problem in the family. But the truth is that the REAL problem is the interaction of the family as a whole in destructive ways. The other family members use the problem person, the identified patient, as an excuse not to focus on what they are doing that is the real source of the tension everyone experiences. The problem person is identified, by the other family members, as the person who is out-of-whack, or 'sick'. The identified patient. (This is also known as 'scape goating'.)

Remember, the whole family is in tension, not just the brothers. Jacob is, Joseph is, and also the sisters, the mothers, etc. etc. It's complex, let me tell you!

But, for the brothers, smack in the middle of this mess, the problem is not Father Jacob's passivity, nor is it their relationship to Jacob or anyone else. The problem is Joseph. And no family can continue with tension like this getting higher and higher without things coming to a breaking point. Something has to give. And it does.

Now his brothers went to pasture their father's flock near Shechem. And Jacob said to Joseph, "Are not your brothers pasturing the flock at Shechem? Come, I will send you to them." Joseph answered, "Here I am." So, Jacob said to him, "Go now, see if it is well with your brothers, and with the flock; and bring word back to me." So, he sent him from the valley of Hebron.

Joseph came to Shechem, and a man found him wandering in the fields; the man asked him, "What are you seeking?" "I am seeking my brothers," he said. "Tell me, please, where they are pasturing the flock." The man said, "They have gone away, for I heard them say, 'Let us go to Dothan.'" So, Joseph went after his brothers and found them at Dothan. They saw him from a distance, and, before he came near to them, they conspired to kill him. They said to one another, "Here comes this dreamer. Come now, let us kill him and throw him into one of the pits; then we shall say that a wild animal has devoured him, and we shall see what will become of his dreams." But when Reuben heard it, he delivered Joseph out of their hands, saying, "Let

us not take his life." Reuben said to his brothers, "Shed no blood; throw him into this pit here in the wilderness but lay no hand on him." He said this so that he might rescue him out of their hand and restore him to their father. So, when Joseph   came to his brothers, they stripped him of his robe, the long robe with sleeves that he wore; and they took him and threw him into a pit. The pit was empty. There was no water in it. Then they sat down to eat. Genesis 37:12-24

His brothers saw him coming. And don't you know, he just HAD to wear that long-sleeved robed his dad had given him. Just HAD to wear it.

And seeing him coming, across the wide fields, wearing that . . . that THING. . . with a grin. . . and a smirk. . . . well, something snapped in the boys.

Can you hear how much frustration and anger are behind the words in the text? How much deep anger bubbling up from a terrible sense of unfairness, unfairness from the one person on the face of the earth who should be fair and supportive of all of the boys, their father.

How often had they fantasized doing harm to the brat. . . to the one who had caused their father to turn against them. . . of course Joseph had done nothing of the kind, this was all Jacob's doing, but I can hear the boys accusing Joseph of this just the same.

They grab him and rip the hated robe off of

him, probably tearing it in several places as they did so. Then they throw him into a pit, probably a dry cistern. Joseph's lucky he didn't break his leg, or his neck, the way they probably tossed him about.

I have to hand it to Reuben. He's the first-born son, the oldest. And he does a very typical first-born child type of thing. Reuben is the more responsible one, always has been, and he's used to ordering his brothers around, and although they gripe and moan and complain about how bossy Reuben is, nevertheless, they usually do what he tells them to do. Because they've learned over the years that usually Reuben is right.

Reuben is mature enough to realize that killing Joseph is not the answer. No matter what he thought of his half-brother, Reuben obviously loved his father, Jacob, even with all of Jacob's faults and the favoritism he showed to Joseph. Reuben knew how much the old man loved Joseph, and Reuben did not want to see his father hurt. He loved his dad, even though he had problems with Jacob, just as all the boys did.

Reuben is a typical first-born in that he is protective of his parents, usually taking their side, though not always, and he is very reluctant to bad-mouth them. Reuben, as first born, is also protective of the whole family, even the BRAT, Joseph. Reuben would probably like nothing better than to be able to knock some sense into the teen, but killing him? No, that's going too far. He's a member of the family, and you don't do that to members of the family.

So, Reuben persuades his brothers to throw Joseph into the empty cistern (a cistern catches rainwater for drinking, etc.), and then he plans to come back later and get Joseph out. All the while he has to be hoping that Joseph would have learned his lesson...

But things don't go quite like Reuben planned.

Looking up, they saw a caravan of Ishmaelites coming from Gilead, with their camels carrying bum, balm and resin, on their way to carry it down to Egypt. Then Judah said to his brothers, "What profit is it if we kill our brother and conceal his blood? Come, let us sell him to the Ishmaelite, and not lay our hands on him, for he is our brother, our own flesh." And his brothers agreed. They drew Joseph up, lifting him out of the pit, and sold him to the Ishmaelites for twenty pieces of silver, and they took Joseph to Egypt.

When Reuben returned to the pit and saw that Joseph was not in the pit, he tore his clothes. He returned to his brothers and said, "The boy is gone; and I, where can I turn?" Then they took Joseph's robe, slaughtered a goat, and dipped the robe in the blood. They had the long robe with sleeves taken to their father, and they said, "This we have found; see now whether it is your son's

robe or not." Jacob recognized it and said, "It is my son's robe! A wild animal has devoured him; Joseph is without doubt torn to pieces." Then Jacob tore his garments and put sackcloth on his loins and mourned for his son many days. All his sons and all his daughters sought to comfort him; but he refused to be comforted and said, "No, I shall go down to Sheol to my son, mourning." Thus, Joseph's father bewailed him. Meanwhile, the Midianites had sold him in Egypt to Potiphar, one of Pharaoh's officials, the captain of the guard. Genesis 37:25-36

For some reason Reuben left the group after Joseph was thrown into the pit. Maybe he had a task to perform away from his brothers while they had lunch.

When he gets back, the brothers have moved on, away from the cistern, and Reuben looks in, prepared to give Joseph a little lecture before he pulls the teen out, and does he get a surprise! Joseph is gone.

When he tracks his brothers down, and they tell him what they have done, Reuben is nearly beside himself. He has not been able to do what is so deep within most first-born children: protect the family. And if you can do this without making people angry at you, so much the better. He'd come up with a pretty decent plan, after all. He knew his brothers would cool off eventually, they always do.

And then, when he was alone, he'd sneak back to the cistern and get his little brother out.

But now? Everything's come apart, and Reuben is frantic. He knows his father will be absolutely crushed; in fact, the old man would probably never get over this loss. It might even kill him. And he, Reuben, was the oldest, he was the responsible one, the one who should have prevented this. Reuben can already see his father's terrible, disappointed, eyes, in agony.

God!!! How can we tell dad?

Well, they did, didn't they? Made up a whopper of a lie, and then used the hated robe to support the lie. They simply could never admit that they had sold their brother, their own brother, into slavery.

They knew, all of them, that if Jacob found out he'd never forgive them, and they'd all be worse off than before. The old man might even try to go to Egypt to find Joseph and rescue him, and that was fruitless. God alone knew what the caravan had really done with Joseph. No, even Reuben could see that the lie was the way to go.

And Reuben was right: Jacob is shattered. All his worse fears have come to pass.

And nobody will speak the truth.

So, what can we learn from all of this? A whole lot, but I want to offer up three things.

First: every family is going to have problems. So, when trials and troubles come our way, remember that family problems are a part of life. Every child is going to mess up, and I mean big time. Every parent is going to mess up, and I mean big time.

Second: favoritism by a parent is bad, and we know this. This is why all of us say, "I don't favor one child over another. I treat all my children equal." Really?

Well, we think we do, and goodness knows, we try. But what do our children have to say about this? Hmmmm.

The truth is we are drawn more to some of our children than others. We perceive a weakness, or a similar way to our way of thinking, or doing something. We are naturally drawn to this child, while although loving the others like crazy, we realize that these others are different from us.

This is natural, even normal. Unchecked, of course, it's bad. But this truth, that we are naturally drawn to one child over another, and, well, our kids know this quite well. Usually they are very vocal about this. But we parents? We have a hard time admitting this. But it's true. Denying this tendency gets us into trouble, and always makes things worse. So, when the brother or sister accuses us of favoring one over another, listen!!! And be prepared to have to eat a bit of humble pie.

Usually, our spouse can help us with this, for the spouse can usually see very well the favoritism by her/his partner. It's seeing one's own actions that's hard.

Third, and perhaps this is the most important thing to take away from this story, is where the story tells us God is. I mean, when troubles come, and one of the worst troubles is a family in crisis that explodes, we wonder where God is. This story gives a beautiful answer: God is in the meanwhile.

Look at verse 36: Meanwhile, Joseph, who was not dead, was sold into slavery in Egypt.

God is already working in Joseph's life and the brother's lives and in Jacob's life. But no one can see it at the time. Which is a great reminder that God's time is different from ours.

Jesus said, "I will not, I will never, ever leave you desolate. The comforter will come." (John 14:18) Turning evil around, not negating the evil, but bringing something good, eventually, from it. . . this takes time.

Jesus rose from the dead, but it was a good while before a lot of people heard about this. In fact, it was years, YEARS!!!

It was years before Joseph changed from a bratty teen and became a completely different person, a mature man who was a great leader.

You may be in a very dark time; your family may be in a very dark time.

Do not despair.

Do not give up hope.

Unknown to everyone, and I mean EVERYONE in this story, God is at work. And he is at work in your life, in your family's life, for Jesus Christ is alive and his Spirit is here, with us, with all of us. And that Spirit is working, working, working. . . even with all that's happened to you and to yours. . . . so much bitterness. . . so much frustration. . .

God is working. . . .unseen. . . unheard. . . for us. . . for we, through Christ, are his precious children, and he loves us with a love that is astounding and wants to help us.

Where is God?

Meanwhile. . . .

The Story of Joseph
How God Works in Our Lives

CHAPTER TWO

Starting to Do Good then WHAM!

Now Joseph was taken down to Egypt, and Potiphar, an officer of Pharaoh, the captain of the guard, an Egyptian, bought him from the Ishmaelites, who had brought him down there.--- Genesis 39: 1

There is no mention of how long Joseph was a slave in Potiphar's house. It could have been a few months, a year, perhaps longer. Notice also that there is no soul searching, not in the biblical text. As a rule, the Bible generally is not that interested in how people feel about things, even about themselves. It's far more interested in what they did.

I think it's a safe bet to assume that as Joseph was in the slave pens, as he started to work for Potiphar, doing the dirtiest jobs that nobody wanted to do (cleaning out the latrines, mucking out what passed for barns among the Egyptian ruling class, so forth and so on), he did a lot of thinking. About how he got where he was, what would happen to him, the chances of him seeing his family again. All he could see at this point was being a slave among other slaves, living in someplace-not-very-nice, completely alone, no hope of escape. I also think, as most of us would if we were in Joseph's place, that he felt like he'd been knifed in the gut by his brother's betrayal of him. There may have been little love lost between Joseph and his brothers, but, for goodness' sake, they were his brothers!!!! They were his family!!!!!! And they had turned on him, betrayed him, basically threw him away to die.

I'm sure he cried himself out, and perhaps was told by other slaves to shut up, quit his blubbering. Joseph had been the pampered one, the 'prince' among his brothers, so to speak. To be jerked away from all of that to where he was now had to have been hard on him. Now he was the lowest of the low. He was, literally, owned by Potiphar. And if he wanted to live, he'd better get used to that. Fast.

He did, and, as with some who are thrown into the fire of hard experience, over time the real Joseph began to emerge

The Lord was with Joseph, and he became a successful man; he was in the house of his Egyptian master. His master saw that the Lord was with him, and that the Lord caused all that he did to prosper in his hands. So, Joseph found favor in his master's sight and attended him. Potiphar made Joseph overseer of his house and put him in charge of all that he had. From the time that he made him overseer in his house and over that he had, the Lord blessed the Egyptian's house for Joseph's sake. The blessing of the Lord was on all that Potiphar had, in house and field. So, Potiphar left all that he had in Joseph's charge; and with Joseph there, he had no concern for anything but the food that he ate. --- Genesis 39: 2-6

Somewhere along the way Joseph lost his brattiness. Maybe it quite literally got knocked out of him by some of the other slaves. Whatever. At some point, Joseph made the decision 'I'm going to survive this!'

I'm alive, he would have said, and I'm in a terrible place, a terrible situation. But I'M ALIVE! And I'm now completely alone, which is definitely scary. I'm not used to being all by myself. Always had my brothers and sisters around me. It's so strange not having them here. But I'm not a kid anymore. I know I've acted like a kid, especially with my brothers. But they're not here. No one is. It's up to me to take care of myself. The Lord has kept me alive, amazingly. So, I guess I can survive. Even as a slave. And maybe. . . just maybe. . . one day. . . freedom.

It takes a lot of courage, sheer guts, for this young man to do what he did. The easy thing would have been to give up, to take his orders, do, not care whether he lived or died, survive, sort of; but that's not what he did. He knew right from wrong. He'd been taught manners. He knew how to shoulder responsibility, even though he didn't do this at home a lot, nevertheless, he still knew what it took to do a job right, to be honest, to follow through on what you said you'd do.

In other word, his character, his integrity, starts to emerge. He shows initiative. He shows he can be trusted with responsibility.

This is what the biblical text is getting at when it says that the Lord was with Joseph and blessed Potiphar's house because of Joseph. Do you think the Lord would bless a young man behaving irresponsibly? Being selfish? Being cruel?

Don't think so. Joseph began to live an honest life of integrity and responsibility, even as a slave among other slaves. He had been taught that that's what good people do and it's what the Lord wants of his people.

Indeed, God blessed Joseph for this and Potiphar's house, that is, his family and servants. Joseph shows that he can be trusted to do a job and do it right. He's perhaps 18, maybe 19.

Anyone who has supervised older teens knows that the ones who do behave right, shoulder responsibility, show honesty to others and taking care to do their jobs as best they can, these older teens stand out from their peers.

Once you recognize such a young adult, what do you do with them? Of course! You give them MORE responsibility because you know that they can handle it. And what's more important, they usually WANT more responsibility, they hunger to engage in such challenges to prove themselves, to stretch themselves.

This is precisely what Potiphar does, and I'm sure it was done gradually. As Joseph did job after job well, respected authority and others, gradually Potiphar gave him more and more responsibility. Until Joseph was over the whole house. He was in charge of everything.

I would say it took at least eight months to a year for this to happen. So, Joseph is probably around 20, maybe 21, when the next part of the story begins.

It's time for some sex.

Now, Joseph was handsome and good-looking. And after a time, his master's wife cast her eyes on Joseph and said, "Lie with me." But he refused and said to his master's wife, "Look, with me here, my master has no concern about anything in the house, and he has put everything that he has in my hand. He is not greater in this house than I am, nor has he kept back anything form me, except yourself, because you are his wife. How then could I do this great wickedness, and sin against God?" And, although she spoke to Joseph day after day, he would not consent to lie beside her or to be with her. --- Genesis 39: 6-10

Whew. . . how did we get into the middle of some steamy,

TV soap opera? Or, is this just the way human beings are?

There is not much detail to this story, which frustrates us, because we want to KNOW! How did this 'thing' with Mrs. Potiphar and Joseph begin? Was it when he served them dinner, and his hand brushed lightly against hers, and she felt a tingle go through her. . .?

Or was it when he accompanied her to market, holding the basket and walking behind her. She noticed all the glances of the other women, their eyes taking in Joseph and then flitting to her, and she could see the envy behind those glances.

This is the territory of the novelist, which my creative imagination would like to explore; however, this is not a novel, so, with a sigh, I must keep close to the text, much as I would like to engage in fancy.

The question the text raises is: why did Joseph refuse?

Character again. He is loyal to the man who first recognized his abilities. He knows he cannot go home, for that's gone forever. His home is in Potiphar's house, where he is respected, where he has a very important job. In fact, he has a future.

No, he is simply not going to put all this in jeopardy.

Joseph acknowledges this, but then he ends his speech to Mrs. Potiphar by saying that adultery is a great wickedness and goes against God.

Where in the world did Joseph learn this? I mean, think about it! There is no temple in this story because the temple would not be built for hundreds of years. In fact, there isn't even a tabernacle, the portable temple (a huge tent) that Moses built for the years the people wandered in the wilderness. The temple and its precursor, the tabernacle, were the centers of the Jewish faith, but they were not yet built and would not be built for hundreds of years.

Maybe more to the point, the Ten Commandments had not yet been given. The commandments were written with the finger of God on Mt. Sinai after Moses led the people out of bondage in Egypt. Sure enough, the seventh commandment is "Do not commit adultery." (Exodus 20: 1-17 and repeated in Deuteronomy 5: 1-21) But Moses and the Ten Commandments are way in the future. Before the temple was built, yes, but still, way in the future.

So, if the written law of God is in the future, then just where did Joseph get the idea that to sleep with some else's spouse is not just a bad idea, but is, in fact, against God's will?

The answer is simple: the young man learned it from his family. That is, knowing this is comes from how he was raised.

Remember, God made a covenant (an agreement wherein one or more parties agree to do something for the other parties) with Abraham, and Abraham's son Isaac, and with Isaac's son Jacob, who was Joseph's father. Jacob taught his family what God had promised to do for his grandfather Abraham, for his father Isaac and for him. Make them a great nation. Although God did not specify exactly what he wanted in return from Abraham, Abraham set the example for his sons and grandchildren and great-grandchildren by accepting God's offer of land and offspring and trusting God to make this happen. This trust was lived out in the family behaving differently from those around them, treating one another differently and worshipping differently. In other words, they would be God's unique, special people, living in a way that separated them from all other people. Thus, their way of life and their very lives were living testimony to the fact that their God, YHWH, was the Living God, that this God intervened in his people's lives. Abraham and his family thus deliberately chose to live differently from others, and this different way of living, with values that were not the same as the people around them, this way of living pleased God.

So, given that the core of the way their family lived, what made the family 'tick' so to speak, was God's covenant with them. They believed that God stood by them and was with them and that God definitely wanted his people, when they too made covenants, to stand by them. Especially when it came to husband and wife. This relationship is the basic unit among human beings. Father, mother and children are the core of the family, and whatever threatens this relationship between husband and wife threatens the family as a whole.

Adultery violates a most solemn covenant that binds a man and woman together in traditional marriage. Adultery threatens the very foundation of the family, the family's livelihood and even ruptures the family as a whole. Indeed, adultery is a great wickedness in the sight of God.

Where and how did Joseph learn this in the family? You know exactly where he learned it. He learned it where you and I did, where all of us did: he learned it at home the way all children learn what's right and what's wrong. He learned it whenever the family gathered and such things might have been discussed, like at the dinner table, or when he was working with his dad outside, or kidding around with his brothers and sisters while they talked about such things. He would have learned it from his mother, as she told him stories about other families and what pleased and didn't please God.

In other words, Joseph was raised to know right from wrong. It was wrong because it violated one of the basic relationships that God wanted for human beings, namely, "that it was not good for the man to be alone." (Genesis 2:18) Man and woman are to be together, wife and husband, husband and wife, helping each other, supporting each other.

Of course, knowing all this has not stopped adultery from happening. The sexual allure, the pull of man to woman,

woman, this deep, deep urge, this yearning to touch the other, to embrace the other, to become united to the other, is within all of us. It is deep and very, very powerful. It is so powerful that sometimes it overpowers us completely; all we can do is dream and think endlessly of being with him, being with her. This yearning is so strong that it can overwhelm the conscious reservations we put up that are to prevent our uniting with the beloved. Thus, the evil of adultery is pushed aside in the onrush of yearning, of desire.

But not with Joseph. He refuses Mrs. Potiphar. He definitely stood out, didn't he? Loyal. Responsible. Sticks to ethical and moral standards. The guy's a real boy-scout, right?

Well... maybe... maybe not... not exactly...

The text says Mrs. Potiphar would not take no for an answer. She kept at the young man day after day after day. Until finally...

One day, however, when he went into the house to do his work, and while no one else was in the house, she caught hold of his garment, saying, "Lie with me!" But he left his garment in her hand and fled and ran outside. When she saw that he had left his garment in her hand and had fled outside, she called out to the members of her household and said to them, "SEE! My husband has brought among us a Hebrew to insult us! He came in to me to lie with me, and I cried out with a loud voice; and when he heard me raise my voice and cry out, he left his garment beside me, and fled outside." The she kept his garment by her until his master came home, and she told him the same story, saying, "The Hebrew servant whom you have brought among us, came in

to me to insult me; but as soon as I raised my voice and cried out, he left his garment beside me and fled outside."--Genesis 39: 11-18

Reading this story as it is usually translated in our Bibles (like in the New Revised Standard Version above) it sounds as if Mrs. Potiphar came close to having her way with Joseph. Poor guy!!! She finally is able get him by herself but he runs away, and all she can grab is his shirt, which she then turns into the most outlandish tale.

For years I thought that was what happened. It is what the text says, right?

Maybe.

You see, the Hebrew word that is translated as' garment' and sometimes 'shirt', has no exact equivalent in English, especially American English. The word refers to a long, shirt-like cloth that was worn underneath other garments, and most often was tied about a man's hips.

Read that last phrase in that sentence just above this one again.

I'll wait.

Think about it. . .

Ah. Now you get it.

The garment in question is something of a combination shorts and T-shirt. It's something you wear next to your skin, and then put other clothes on it and then its secured around the man's hips. If it's unsecured, if it's untied, then that means someone had to have untied it. Because to get at this particular article of clothing, and for Mrs. Potiphar to be holding it tightly as Joseph pulled away means (1) that Joseph's outer garments had to have been discarded and (2) his undergarment was untied, was loose. Was completely open. Think of a hospital gown in reverse. A hospital gown is tied in the back. Flip it around so it's untied in the front. That's what's going on here. Completely open.

This might seem a real stretch to interpret the text this way but consider something else the text says that we usually just read as background information. The text says that "One day, when Joseph went into the house to do his work, and while no one else was in the house. . . "

Question: who's in charge of the household staff?

Joseph.

Then who would be the one to schedule who is doing what in the house?

Joseph.

The only way for not servants to be in the house is because Joseph scheduled it that way.

Remember, Mrs. Potiphar is not in charge of the household staff, Joseph is. (Remember how amazingly patriarchal cultures were then in the middle east) Usually the wife of the Great Man Who Owns the House is thought of as being in charge of the house. Still, it is a wise wife who knows how to utilize societal conventions, and so most likely she would have told Joseph what she wanted done in the house on a particular day leaving it to him to organize the staff so that her orders would be carried out. The staff ordinarily take their day-to-day operating instructions from Joseph, not from Mrs. Potiphar.

Still, she could have requested that everyone be gone; but staff being staff, they would have quietly checked with Joseph to make sure this was all right with him, the real boss, before they took off.

Botom line: there's no way ALL staff would be gone

from the house for the day and Joseph NOT know this. He did NOT show up for work and exclaim, oh my goodness, where is everyone? What's happened to them?

Was ordering all staff to take the day off something that happened frequently in this household? Don't know, but I think it would be doubtful that this happened much. More to the point, when Mrs. Potiphar gave the order for the staff to not be in the house was this something that happened that morning or did she give this order the previous evening? Does this matter?

Perhaps not, yet it does prompt intriguing speculation. If Joseph was ordered that morning to send the staff home, or the staff was sent home before Joseph entered the house, then he very well could have been surprised by Mrs. Potiphar's actions. However, if he received orders from her the night before to make sure there were no staff present the next morning, then if he didn't know what she was probably going to do, he is a seriously stupid young man. And Joseph, son of Jacob, was not a stupid young man. Therefore, if he had received such orders and showed up for work the next day, knowing full well what would probably happen, hmmmmmm.

I know, I know, he had no choice about showing up, he was a slave, and he could have simply resisted any action by Mrs. Potiphar, holding his hands up, palms out, saying No, No, please don't do this!!!!!

Having been an actor I will grant that this 'scene' could very well be played in two, more or less, opposing ways: Joseph resisting, Joseph not resisting. Both could be true to the text as it is given.

Nevertheless, I believe that Joseph was more complicit in this situation than most people have been willing to believe. I've come to believe this because (1) Joseph, due to his position in the household, would very likely have known about the staff holiday, plus (2) there's what the text says about his undergarment, namely that Mrs. Potiphar is just holding it. Nothing is said about the garment being ripped or torn. To be holding this piece of clothing after Joseph fled means that it slipped off Joseph's shoulders as he ran away. If it had remained tied, and she had been holding it, it would have ripped when the young man bolted from the room. There's also a third reason that I'll present in a page or two.

All of this is rich soil for novelists, and we can enjoy such fiction about this situation, but only so long as we realize that depicting what went on with Mrs. Potiphar and Joseph is just that: fiction. Remember, the biblical text is silent on this. What I do know is that Joseph was a man, a young man, and that he had been the object of Mrs. Potiphar's attention for some time. I doubt that a woman such as Mrs. Potiphar would have been drawn to a naive schoolboy over such a span of several months if there had been nothing to encourage her. I do think that's why she kept on, beyond just a week or two. His voice and even his body said no, but his eyes. . . ah, his eyes. . . they were a whole different story.

I do think that finally they had come to agreement, and things were worked out. The staff is scheduled in such a way that Joseph and Mrs. Potiphar have the place to themselves. Potiphar is who-knows-where. The two of them are alone at last! After months!!!!

And now she's sitting on her bed, holding his undergarment in her hands as she hears him running away through the empty house. She had to have blinked several times. What just happened? He was right here. RIGHT HERE!!! GOD! ALL OF HIM!!!!

Did he just turn his back on me. ON ME???????????

She stands up, and a cold fury begins to build inside her. I'm being spurned by a. . . by a boy? A BOY? What an arrogant, conceited puppy!!!!!!! Turn your back on me!!!!

Well, Mr. HIGH-and-MIGHTY-and-PURE Joseph, you need to be taught a lesson on just who's really in charge around here! Embarrass me? Make me the butt of my friends' jokes that they whisper to their husbands in the evening??????? Oh no. No, no, no, no, no, no, no, no, no, NO!!!!! You need to learn a lesson, Mr. Joseph! You need to know once and for all just who it is you're dealing with!!!!!! You need to learn who's REALLY in charge around here!!!!!!!!!

When his master heard the words that his wife spoke to him, saying, "This is the way your servant treated me," Potiphar became enraged. And Joseph's master took him and put him in the prison, the place where the king's prisoners were confined; Joseph remained there in prison. ---Genesis 39: 19-20

Potiphar felt betrayed.

Last one to know, right? Probably every servant in the household was aware that Mrs. Potiphar had the hots for Joseph. They probably were not terribly surprised to get their day off.

When he hears his wife tell her lie Potiphar explodes. And, did you notice? Mrs. Potiphar actually blamed her husband for this whole episode. "The Hebrew whom YOU have brought among us, came in to insult me."

I can hear her. "He attempted to RAPE me Potiphar!!! RAPE ME!!!!! YOUR SERVANT!!!! The one YOU put in charge of the house! He's the one who does the servants' schedules! No one was here. That's why no one came when I called, and believe you me, I screamed my head off. But no one heard me BECAUSE NO ONE WAS AROUND! He got scared because I screamed and fought. I'm not easy!!!!! He ran off, finally!!!!!!"

If I can get my husband focused on Joseph, get him to blame Joseph totally, get him enraged so he's not thinking straight, I can lead him to where I want him to go like I lead my dog. . .

Lady Macbeth had nothing on Mrs. Potiphar.

In those days for a slave to attack, nearly rape the wife of a royal official is an automatic death sentence. Joseph is a dead man.

Everything he had, his nice room, good food, the esteem among other servants, all gone. And he had done nothing to deserve such judgment. Well. . . almost nothing.

Why didn't Potiphar just take Joseph out and kill him? Actually, that's a fairly good question, and, truthfully, I don't have an answer to it. The biblical text does not say. Which makes me mighty curious.

Potiphar was within his rights to do this, to kill the young man. No one would have questioned him. Slaves had no rights. None. Their lives were in the hands of their masters to do with as they pleased.

So why didn't Potiphar kill Joseph?

Don't know. But I can make an educated guess. Potiphar obviously liked Joseph. A lot. And he trusted Joseph. A lot. Joseph had good sense, and he was very responsible. I think, first and foremost, Potiphar just did not want to kill this young man that he was so fond of.

It could be that by the time Potiphar found Joseph, either in his room, or somewhere else, that he'd had time to cool down a bit, and to think. Potiphar's not dumb. You don't rise to the position he did at court by being dumb. To have a position at court also means that Potiphar knew something about politics, and therefore he knew a thing or two about how people tick. Plus, he knew his wife. Although he obviously had not connected the dots about his wife and Joseph, as he calmed down he had to have wondered just how such a thing could have happened, and then certain things began to fall into place. Things he'd discounted. No man wants to think his wife is planning to betray him with another lover. But it's always something that's in the back of most guys minds. We tamp it down most of the time, but it never quite goes away, does it?

I think it's entirely possible that by the time he confronted Joseph Potiphar had come to realize that it takes two to tango, and that maybe, just maybe, his wife hadn't told him what really happened. He probably asked Joseph what happened. He was probably still mad, still hurt, but I think that Potiphar also listened to Joseph.

No, he wouldn't kill the young man, but he did want him gone. He wanted him nowhere near his wife. He wanted the young man some place where neither she nor Joseph could ever make contact with one another. He also knew that every servant in the house knew both what had really happened and what his wife was saying, and so would everyone else in the city come the next day. To save what face he could, he had to take action.

And he did.

But he didn't kill Joseph.

Knowing a bit about Joseph now, how he was honest, respectful, responsible, to realize how close he came to slipping had to have made him very ashamed of himself. The Lord helped me, raised me up to a position of responsibility, and I blow it completely. Suicide may have flitted through his mind. But he held on.

He was right back where he started from, all those months ago. But he was alive. And somehow, someway, God gave him the strength to hold on.

But the Lord was with Joseph and showed him steadfast love; he gave him favor in the sight of the

chief jailer. The chief jailer committed to Joseph's care all the prisoners who were in the prison, and whatever was done there, he was the one who did it. The chief jailer paid no heed to anything that was in Joseph's care, because the Lord was with him; and whatever he did, the Lord made it prosper.---Genesis 39: 21-23

Steadfast love. Those two words are used a lot in the bible of God. They've become so familiar, though, that it may be difficult to really get at what they mean. We sometimes use phrases as 'never ending love', or 'eternal love', but they have their own difficulties.

Let me paraphrase what it means. God's steadfast love means that there is nothing you can do, absolutely nothing, NOTHING, that will ever cause God to stop loving us. No matter what.

Isn't it interesting that the biblical text specifically says that God's steadfast love was with Joseph when he went to prison? What I mean is that most of us wouldn't think of the steadfast love of God coming into play here because Joseph was jailed unjustly. He'd done nothing wrong! God's justice, God's righteousness, will uphold Joseph, give him strength to endure unjust persecution. Yes it will. It could be interpreted as simply the text indicating that God had not abandoned Joseph, that God was still with him. It's just that throughout the Old Testament, particularly among the prophets, when they proclaim God's steadfast love to Israel, God's own people, it's always in reference to the people sinning, turning away from God and to other gods, doing so many things that displease and anger God. Yet, proclaim the prophets, God's steadfast love for Israel endures forever. The context where, in the Old Testament, this phrase, God's steadfast love, occurs is most often within the context of a person(s) sinning, departing from God's ways, prompting God's displeasure, even anger, which then is somewhat countered by the prophets remembering God's love for his people does not evaporate.

Given that Joseph has done no wrong, that he is a victim of injustice, that the text says nothing about God's justice shall eventually prevail, that God will vindicate this righteous young man and reveal that his punishment is unjust. The text does not say this, which is, once you think of it, somewhat odd. Instead, it speaks of God's never-ending, forgiving love.

Why?

I think it's because Joseph, knowing he almost slipped, was incredibly harsh with himself about this, blaming himself unmercifully. The text declaring that God's 'steadfast love' is with Joseph, is that third reason I mentioned that I believe Joseph was more complicit in what happened with Mrs. Potiphar than tradition has taught.

Remember, Joseph was the favored child, the one his dad doted on, the one who was smart, and the one who was supposed to be better than his brothers. But here he had gone and behaved just like some of his cruder brothers.

For people who have a conscience, who know better, who think of themselves as different from others, perhaps even better than others, committing or even nearly committing a great wrong can be shattering. One's basic image of oneself is torn apart, and what's left is deeply disturbing, even painful to contemplate.

I think Joseph entered such a dark period within himself. There's nothing about this in the text, save that one reference to God's steadfast love being shown to Joseph. The text could simply mean that God was looking after Joseph in prison, and this makes perfect sense too.

Perhaps I'm making too much of 'God's steadfast love'

here. Perhaps. All I know is that this phrase, something that names the very essence of God, is so often used in the psalms and prophets. The psalmists and the prophets point out the people's sins and proclaim that God's judgment shall come. But then, so many, many times, they will refer to God's steadfast love enduring forever in spite of the peoples' sins. (See especially Psalm 137, Psalm 118 and Psalm 107)

I have come to think that in this text the Bible is teaching us that God's forgiving love was with Joseph, helping him, in spite of Joseph's own self-condemnation. Joseph came to realize that even though he was involved in what happened to him, nevertheless, the fault lay far more with Mrs. Potiphar (and Mr. Potiphar).

I think that Joseph fought a great, internal battle within himself, a soul battle, that went on throughout the first weeks and then months of his imprisonment. I say this because the biblical text says that Joseph eventually came to be respected by the jailer. He earned this respect by being, once again, responsible, by treating others fairly, honestly, with justice, even in prison. And, as before, this took time. Over time Joseph's real character began to come to the surface again. God strengthened Joseph to act this way once again. God nurtured Joseph, giving him strength to do the right thing, even there in prison. Again. This was Joseph's bedrock, the knowledge and the experience that God was with him in that dark, dark place. This was what got him through.

Remember this when you go through a dark time.

"God's steadfast love endureth forever," says the Psalmist, and this is so very, very true.

But, because of what we've done, because we did not control ourselves as we should have, we tend to think that God has left us.

Not true.

We do not have a high priest who is unable to sympathize with our weaknesses, but we have one who in every respect has been tested as we are, yet without sin. Let us therefore approach the throne of grace with boldness, so that we may receive mercy and find grace to help in time of need.---Hebrews 4: 15-16

Jesus has been right where you are. He has experienced personal betrayal, abandonment by friends, his enemies triumphant. He has experie3nced physical pain that equals anything any of us could experience.

He knows what it's like and he can help you make it through.

Our tendency is to believe this is true, but ONLY IF WE ARE TREATED BADLY AND WHAT'S HAPPENING TO US IS NOT OUR FAULT IN ANY WAY. When we have messed up, crossed the line, and now have to deal with the consequences of our actions, we Christians tend to think God, Jesus Christ our Lord, is somewhere else. We're on our own because we believe that this is God's justice in action.

It is true that to grow into maturity we need to learn to bear the consequences of our actions. And this can be painful, to put it mildly.

But the challenge to all of us is to never give up hope. And this story about Joseph, especially the way it ends at this point, wonderfully illustrates that God goes with us into our personal darkness, even when such a journey is partially, perhaps even totally, our fault. God is still with us.

So, remember who has you, who is with you. Remember

that God will help you through, leading you, eventually, out of where you are, even when you believe that there is no way out. Yes, you might have to stay in this particular dark place for a good while. But Jesus will be with you the whole time. He will help you bear up under what you're going through. He will enable you to endure what you have to endure.

He will do this because Jesus embodies within himself God's steadfast love. In whatever darkness you're going through, God's steadfast love for you endures forever.

Whenever your cry, "What have I done that this is happening to me? I made a small mistake, and all this happens? Oh, God! Where are you?"

We have not one who simply cannot sympathize with our weakness, NO! What we have is one who in all ways has been tested, just as we all have been, yet he is without sin. So let us approach the throne of grace with boldness, (that is, pray, and pray a lot!) SO THAT we may receive mercy (forgiveness for what we have done, ALL OF IT!) and find grace (steadfast love) to help us keep on going.

The bottom line is simply this: Jesus is with you. Jesus has you close. Jesus will help you endure and make it through the dark time you're going through.

The Story of Joseph
How God Works in Our Lives

CHAPTER THREE

In The Dark

There are times when we go along, mind our own business, try to do what's right and then BOOM! Our life starts to slide down into a pit and everything is chaos.

These are the times when we wonder whether or not there even IS a God, much less whether or not he's with us.

What the scriptures teach, over and over and especially here in this text, is that in every circumstance, even in the most awful of times, we are still in God's loving hands.

One of the worst experiences of such chaos is for trusted friends or family to turn against you. These are the people who are supposed to be the supports that help us cope with the hurricanes of life. When they are gone, things get bad. This is where Joseph is.

Joseph's master took him and put him into the prison, the place where the king's prisoners were confined; he remained there in prison.---Genesis 39: 20

Dark places come in all shapes and sizes, don't they? What's common is that they all give us a feeling of being abandoned, a feeling of being all alone. Your marriage has gone, for example, or a close friend(s) has preferred listening to half-truths, even lies, rather than the real truth and has withdrawn from you. Or maybe you're having to move through one of the worst feelings of chaotic darkness: your child has turned against you. Gone against your values, the things you've tried to stress, the things you've lived by for years. Or perhaps the worst of all: your child, your beloved daughter, your beloved son, has died. An accident, a terrible car accident perhaps, or bad fentanyl laced the drug taken and your child is gone because of an accidental 'overdose'. Perhaps a medical condition that had been hidden for a long time suddenly erupts, taking your son or daughter.

Am I ever going to get through this? I can't stop thinking about things, I can NOT shut my mind off, GOD!!!!!!! It hurts so much. . .

Grieving is hard, and all of us do it differently. And it doesn't help for our friends to say that we're at stage one or stage two of Kubler-Ross' stages of grief. HOW COULD THEY KNOW ANYTHING OF WHAT I'M GOING THROUGH!!!!!!!!!

As a pastor I have been amazed, at times, at the insensitivity of friends and family to the grieving one. Don't they know how what they say will be heard? Are they that dense? Yes, they are.

Most people have a great deal of difficulty putting themselves in the grieving person's position, that is, anticipating or imagining how what is said will be heard, what feelings might arise from the words and tone of voice. Some people can do this, but for most it's beyond them. There is no fault in this. Not a bit. And if you realize you have trouble doing this, please, do not become severely critical of yourself. Just honestly admit this, to yourself most of all. It's refusing to recognize this that gets us into trouble. We say something that we thought would be comforting and it certainly is not received that way. So, we get hurt, and just a bit later, angry, thinking (and perhaps even saying) "Hey, I was only trying to help!"

Yes, and usually our hurting friend or family member

will recognize this in time. But for the moment we stand around very awkwardly, knowing that we've only made things worse, and we certainly did not want to do that.

I've said that some people can put themselves into other's shoes, so to speak, and realize something of the hurt that is going through our friend or family member. If you can do this, good for you. You have a gift. Nevertheless, I have found, in working with people are in deep, serious grief, that saying "I know what you're going through," is the last thing anyone needs to say to the grieving person. You may, indeed, have an idea of what the person is experiencing (through your own past grief, or you're simply very empathic), but the truth is you don't know. You do not know precisely what the other person is feeling. You may think you do, but you do not. You don't for a very simple reason: you are not that other person. Only that other person knows what they're feeling. You may have an idea of it, you may have experienced your own grief some time ago, or you watched and tried to help your parent or your sibling go through their grief, but still, you do not know what this other person is actually going through.

The best way to help a hurting friend going through grief is to admit this, admit it to ourselves and to our friend, saying something like "I don't know what you're going through, but I can see that it really, really hurts." And, honestly, truthfully, the one thing I've learned in all the years I've been a pastor, is that the best thing we can do for such a friend, such a family member, is simply to be with that person, to listen if they want to talk. To be by their side if they don't want to talk. If they're angry, let them be angry. If they're confused, let them be confused. If they want to cry, let them cry. Let them be who they are in these moments.

I'll admit that sometimes it's hard to be with people when they are captive to such powerful, disturbing emotions. Being around a person who is feeling such powerful emotions is not easy. If they are talkative, it doesn't take long for us to begin to feel uncomfortable. We can even start to feel upset ourselves, to the point that we want to get away from our loved one. But believe me, if our loved one begins unburdening herself, himself to us and disturbing emotions are coloring things, then one of the best, most powerful things we can do to help is to take the torrent being unleashed. I mean letting the person speak, and go on speaking, and we do not say anything to stop the person. Often, we might have to bite our tongues to keep still.

So often when such things happen between friends, between family members, we blurt out "You shouldn't feel that way!" Why do we say that? Why SHOULDN'T our friend, our brother, our sister, our spouse, our parent, our child feel this way? It IS how they're feeling right then and there.

We forget that feelings are what they are. In and of themselves they are neutral; it's what we're feeling at a given moment in time. For the most part, we cannot control our feelings, contrary to what a whole lot of teachers (both public school and Sunday school) have told us over the years. Feelings arise spontaneously within us as we interact with our environment and the people around us. Feelings are also, generally speaking, fleeting. They don't last, they come, they go. They're intense and then they diminish.

Whenever we blurt out "You shouldn't feel that way!", or "It's not right to feel like that!" we're admitting that what was said to us has prompted a reaction inside of us, a feeling of alarmed surprise, or real concern, or sometimes even disgust. We don't like feeling what we're feeling and so we try to stop what's making us feel bad: we want to make our friend cease talking. We want to shut them up.

Does this help our friend, our family member? Uh, no.

For all of us, the appropriate concern is whether or not feelings are acted on. Just feeling angry at our spouse, for instance, REALLY ANGRY, so much so that we blurt out to a friend, "I'd like to murder him/her!!!!!" means little in and of itself. If we then begin to take steps to do what we've blurted out, that's different.

Ruth Bell Graham, wife of evangelist Billy Grahm is famous for her reply to a question asked during an interview on TV. "Have you ever considered divorce, Mrs. Graham?" Ruth was sitting beside her husband. Without batting an eye, and with no hesitation she said, "No, but I've considered murder several times." The audience laughed and Dr. Graham smiled, but it wasn't a big smile. It was a sheepish and embarrassed smile. Ruth smiled too and held her head high. Marriage is hard. Marriage, EVERY marriage has its dark times. Every family goes through dark times. Even the family of the most famous preacher of the twentieth century.

I use that little example because all of us have been involved with people who have frustrated us, made us furious about something, and we've blurted such words when we've later talked with friends. Our friends, knowing quite well we have no intention of committing first-degree murder, just nod along with us and say "Uh-huh". We who are friends with the person who said this realize that this is just a way of letting off steam, of relieving emotional pressure that's been building up inside us.

As we all know if pressure builds up, if it's not decreased in some way, then an explosion will happen. The person going through grief builds up a lot of emotional pressure, and the best friends are those who are willing to allow this emotional pressure to be released, along with watching to see that the grieving person's behavior does not become self-destructive.

My own personal golden rule in being with those grieving is first and foremost, simply listen. Keep my responses very limited. Listen to this person, really listen. And then say something like, "Wow. . . there's a lot going on, isn't there?" Then when the other nods back we can say "It still hurts." Not a question but a statement. Framing this as a question will prompt our friend to say yes or no, and perhaps the conversation then ends. It's more helpful to let the other person know that we are with them, that we recognize what the other person is obviously experiencing, namely pain. For the grieving person to encounter a friend who recognizes, even partially, the world the griever is inhabiting, really helps. It's very much like a cup of cold water on a hot, humid, draining day.

And, if you are the loved one I'm writing about, if you are the one who is in a dark, dark place, I want to say something that I have learned, both from others and from my own walk through life, if you are going through a dark, very difficult time, and especially if you have lost someone very special and your grief is immense, then please, be gentle with yourself.

There are always going to be some people who will say things that, although meant to be comforting, meant to be helpful, end up prompting doubts about how you're coping, prompting concerns about your actually being able to get through what you're going through. These people seem to some sort of expectation of you, some sort of expected behavior that you are not giving them.

Above all, you yourself, after a while, begin to criticize what you're doing, how you're coping or not coping. I should be doing better! I should be able to do these things that I was doing before everything happened! I've tried, and I can't! Oh, I'm so weak, I'm just not any good at all!!!!! To no one!!!!!

And on, and on, and on. For those of us who either by birth order, or through our natural internal wiring, are predisposed to be highly responsible, these thoughts and feelings of inadequacy can really do a number on us. We perceive ourselves as not living up to our own, internal expectations, making us incredibly frustrated at ourselves. Why can't I get through this??????

Please hear these words: Be gentle with yourself.

What you're going through is incredibly difficult, and everybody goes through grief and hard days differently. It takes time, lots of time.

Be gentle with yourself. And ask your closest friends and close family to be as well. Tell them you're doing your best, that you're doing what you can.

The challenge, obviously, is that we will ourselves to be open to suggestions about what we should do, for sometimes we do get stuck in grief. As a pastor I have listened to the concerns of friends and family about their loved one who lost their spouse, their child. I always ask them to explain what prompts their concern (that is, why call the pastor about this), and so often the reason is not so much the grief of the loved one as it is the unacknowledged grief of the caller.

I do have a basic criterion about all of this, though. And it's one year. One full year. If the loved one is still in deep grief after a year, has not 'moved on' very much at all, then perhaps a helping hand is needed, such as counseling, a grief-support group (which I recommend to everyone who has experienced a significant loss). It's wise to check with a trained counselor about all of this, and I as a minister and not a counselor, refer parishioners to such when, after meeting with the person, I begin to perceive that he or she needs more than two or three sessions. Sometimes I have found that the person is stuck simply because feelings of anger or shame associated with the deceased have not been acknowledged, nor have they ever been expressed. A trained counselor can quite literally be a godsend in such occasions. Let me emphasize that: a trained counselor, one with a PC (Professional Counselor, as certified by the state of residence of the counselor) by the name. I also have particular respect for those Licensed Clinical Social Workers (LCSW) who are also PCs, because such individuals have really helped me personally.

I could say a great deal more about all of this but doing so would take us seriously away from the Joseph story. So, let's get back to the biblical text.

Some time after this, the cupbearer of the king of Egypt and his baker offended their lord the king of Egypt. Pharao was angry with his two officers, the chief cupbearer and the chief baker, and he put them in custody in the house of the captain of the guard, in the prison where Joseph was confined. The captain of the guard charged Joseph with them, and he waited on them; and they continued for some time in custody.---Genesis 40: 1-4

You would think that such 'political' prisoners would have absolutely nothing to do with a lowly Hebrew slave. And ordinarily you'd be right. But remember, at the end of Chapter 39 in Genesis the Biblical narrator tells us that Joseph was put in charge of all of the prisoners because the chief jailer was impressed with Joseph. Joseph was responsible; he was honest; he could be depended on to follow through with orders and carry them out consistently. So gradually, more and more responsibility came Joseph's way.

Let's be honest here. The strength to continue doing the right thing when it's hard to do so, when we're really hurting, does not come solely from within ourselves. It is God's Spirit giving us strength; God does not abandon us.

We may feel as if God has gone far away but we know from Christ, who went into his own dark time of abandonment, of suffering, we know that through his suffering God is with us in our suffering. There is no pain, no hurt that is foreign to the Lord because Jesus, a human being just like us, suffered the torments of hell, just as we do. Jesus took these experiences with him when he ascended into heaven and became united once again with the Father. When this happened all his experiences, all his memories, became part of God himself.

God has sent part of himself, his Spirit to his people (particularly the Prophets and Holy men and women) throughout the Old Testament. But now, after Christ's death and resurrection and ascension God bestows his spirit to all who follow him. This is what Pentecost is all about (Acts 2). The Spirit of God now resonates with Jesus Himself, including all of what happened to Jesus, all of what he went through on earth. His hurts, his pains, his disappointments, his joys, his laughter, all is now part of God and therefore part of the Spirit that touches us.

This is why, when we are in the dark, when we are feeling so low and something inside us, deep inside us, prompts us to cry out to God, we oh-so-faintly acknowledge that there is something outside of our consciousness that is adjacent to our consciousness. What is 'vibrating' (for want of a better term) there prompts a similar vibration within us. That is, the Spirit of God touches us in a way known only to God and somehow, deep, deep, deep inside us, we are strangely comforted, assured. Somehow, we see and feel a bit of light, faint, yes, but still light, coming to us in our darkness.

God himself is with us, touching out consciousness with his presence, letting us know that we are not alone, that we are not in the dark by ourselves. He is with us. And somehow, known only to God, somehow our energy to keep on going, maybe faintly, maybe just barely, but still keeping on going, somehow, we do that. One day at a time. Perhaps one hour at a time. We keep on going. We may be afraid, even terrified. Yet there is also a presence with us that begins to calm our fears. We may lash out with complaints and attacks because we are afraid. Then this same presence that is there one second and only faintly felt the next and the next not at all and then faintly felt again, this presence nevertheless begins to affect us, and we find that terrible, paralyzing fear loosening its death grip on us. After a while we even begin to feel a bit of peace within ourselves, even while we still feel a lot of fear, so that we lessen our lashing out at others.

One night the cup bearer and the baker both dreamed, each his own dream, and each dream with its own meaning. When Joseph came to them in the morning he saw that they were troubled. So, he asked Pharaoh's officers, who were with him in custody in his master's house, "Why are your faces downcast today?"

The said to him, "We have had dreams and there is no one to interpret them."

And Joseph said to them, "Do not interpretations belong to God? Please tell them to me."

So, the chief cupbearer told his dream to Joseph, and said to him, "In my dream there was a vine before me, and on the vine there were three branches. As soon as it budded its blossom came out and the clusters ripened into grapes. Pharaoh's cup was in my hand; and I took the grapes and pressed them into Pharaoh's cup and placed the cup in Pharaoh's hand."

Then Joseph said to him, "This is its interpretation; the three branches are three days. Within three days Pharaoh will lift up your head

and restore you to your office, and you shall place Pharaoh's cup in his hand, just as you used to do when you were the cupbearer. But remember me when it is well with you; please do me the kindness to make mention of me to Pharaoh, and so get me out of this place. For in fact, I was stolen out of the land of the Hebrews; and here also I have done nothing that they should have put me into this dungeon."

When the chief baker saw that the interpretation was favorable, he said to Joseph, "I also had a dream; there were three baskets on my head, and in the uppermost basket there were all sorts of baked food for Pharaoh, but the birds were eating it out of the basket on my head."

And Joseph answered, "This is its interpretation: the three baskets are three days; within three days Pharaoh will lift up your head-from you!-and hang you on a pole; and the birds will eat the flesh from you."

And on the third day, which was Pharaoh's birthday, he made a feast for all his servants, and lifted up the head of the chief cupbearer and the head of the chief baker among his servants. He restored the chief cupbearer to his cupbearing and placed the cup in Pharaoh's hand; but the chief baker he hanged just as Joseph had interpreted to them.

Yet the chief cupbearer did not remember Joseph, but forgot him.---Genesis 40: 5-23

Dreams are important and need to be listened to because they can tell us things about ourselves that often enable us to cope better. Sometimes they even lead us to change our lives. That has actually happened with me.

I have learned so much from the great Swiss psychologist Carl Jung and from Christian writers/counselors who have applied his insights within a Christian framework. The writings of Father Victor white and counselors Morton Kelsay and John Sanford (both of whom are ordained Episcopal priests) have been a tremendous help to me. I commend them to you. (See the bibliography)

As our text says, all true dream interpretation ultimately comes from God. God blessed Joseph with the ability to interpret dreams. Remember his dreams when he was a young boy? About how his father and brothers would bow before him? Now he gives his gifts of dream interpretation to the two men the Lord had brought to him.

The Lord is constantly doing this, you know; putting us into contact with people who need our help (and I'm not talking about just giving handouts). I'm convinced that some of the greatest opportunities of our caring for others occur when we are in the pits and willing to help others even when we are in such a place. It helps so much simply to be able listen to others who are hurting, listening to what is going on in their troubled souls. By willing ourselves to be quiet for a time about our own hurts and being willing to listen, not talk so much, just listen, this can be an amazing gift we can provide to a friend or family member.

And it can help us as well, because I can tell you from my own experience how much we begin to feel better when we cease focusing on ourselves and focus on others for a while.

Joseph told the cupbearer and baker what their dreams

meant, one good, one bad. Joseph told the truth. In addition, he made one small request: remember me.

Hopefully, he would get out of this dark place! Who could blame him? And it makes sense: the cupbearer would remember that young Hebrew who told him the correct interpretation of the dream! He'd remember and then he'd tell Pharoah and then Joseph would get out! Right?

Yet the chief cupbearer did not remember Joseph, but forgot him.---Genesis 40: 23

WHAT??????

This guy Joseph helped, his 'friend', forgot him??????? How could he forget Joseph after what he had done for the cupbearer?

Isn't this, though, what all too often happens? How could she forget me? How could he forget me? After all we've been through? After all I've done for him, for her?

The sad truth is that once most of us feel safe and secure, once we have our needs met, then, being the selfish people that we are, we tend to return to our SOP, our Standard Operating Procedure. Which is focusing on me and mine way more than on anyone else, and so quickly forgetting the needs of others. Even others who helped us.

That's just people. That's just life.

Joseph is experiencing this to the full.

Like Joseph, we may find ourselves in our own dark places for quite a while. On TV and in the movies when the lead character(s) go through tough times they come out of them fairly quickly. The movie has to end, and the TV series has to break and come back next week; even the multi-episode limited series has to come to an end eventually.

But in real life things can just drag on forever!

What do we do in such times? Joseph gives us a clue: take it one day at a time. Do what you can to be true to yourself and to the Lord Jesus Christ. One step at a time. One day at a time. Joseph did not give up on being who he was, on being honest, on carrying out his responsibilities even in prison. He kept on going. Even when there seemed to be no hope, he kept on living.

As many great people throughout Christian history have taught us, affliction is so often the way God works on us so that we become something more than what we were. It's not that hard to be good, trusting, hopeful and loving when life is good, when things are going our way, the bills are paid, it's just great! But what about when the storms come, and it's difficult to pay the bills, and we feel very, very alone? Where is our faith then? Does God cease to be God? Does Jesus go somewhere else?

The Psalmist writes:
Why are you cast down, O my soul, and why do you sigh within me? Put your hope in God. I shall praise him yet, my savior, my God.---Psalm 42: 5

There are times when all we can do is to hold on, just hold on.

Let me repeat that, because it's crucial to get this into our consciousness: there are times when all we can do is to hold on, to just hold on. What we're going through is not just a storm, it's a hurricane, and our little boat, our life, maybe even our family as well, is getting seriously beat up by the howling winds and gigantic waves we're having to make our way through. We feel as if we're drowning. All we can do is to hold on.

Save me, O God, for the waters are up to my neck!---Psalm 73: 1

Even the Apostle Paul went through such a time.

We do not want you to be unaware, brothers and sisters, of the affliction we experienced in Asia; for we were so utterly, unbearable crushed that we despaired of life itself. Indeed, we felt that we had received the sentence of death so that we would rely not on ourselves but on God who raises the dead! He who rescued us from so deadly a peril will continue to rescue us. On Him we have set our hope that he will rescue us again."---II Corinthians 1: 18-10

Even in the darkest times God is with us. Living through such dark times is when we realize that we cannot rely on ourselves anymore. We are used up. Our strength is drained away. We are exhausted. There is no hope.

In such times we become open to that mysterious, obscure sense of presence that is near.

This presence gives us hope when we have no hope.

This presence is light in the midst of the darkness we experience.

In him (Jesus) is life, and this life is the light of the world. This light shines in the darkness, and the darkness shall never overcome it.---John 1: 5.

Because Jesus is with us, the darkness will not overcome us.

The Story of Joseph

How God Works in Our Lives

CHAPTER FOUR

FINALLY, Moving On

Joseph is in Pharaoh's dungeon, forgotten, all alone. He has had to endure this dark place for well over two, maybe even two and a half years. That's a long time to have to experience such darkness. It very well could have left Joseph embittered, bitter. Instead, it became a period of testing, a period of refinement. I think we can say that something, someone, was with Joseph through all of this, helping him with his bitter feelings so that they did not engulf him completely.

After two whole years Pharaoh dreamed that he was standing by the Nile, and there came up out of the Nile seven sleek and fat cows, and they grazed in the reed grass. Then seven other cows, ugly and thin, came up out of the Nile after them, and stood by the other cows on the bank of the Nile. The ugly and thin cows ate up the seven sleek and fat cows. And Pharaoh awoke. Then he fell asleep and dreamed a second time; seven ears of grain, plump and good, were growing on one stalk. Then seven ears, thin and blighted by the east wind, sprouted after them. The thin ears swallowed up the seven plump and full ears. Pharaoh awoke and it was a dream. In the morning his spirit was troubled; so he sent and called for all the magicians of Egypt

and all its wise men. Pharaoh told them his dreams, but there was no one who could interpret them to Pharaoh.---Genesis 41: 1-8

Can you imagine such nightmares? Carnivorous cows in one and then carnivorous plants in the other?????!!! John Carpenter would have had a real party with this. I can see thin, emaciated cows ambling along to another healthy cow and, as the emaciated one approaches, it opens its mouth to reveal not the flat, squarish teeth of the normal, plant-eating cow but the long, pointed, sharp teeth of a predator, rows and rows of them!!!! The poor, healthy cow doesn't stand a chance and is quickly consumed. The plants would be even worse, with the stalks of wheat having a whole lot of small but deadly mouths, mostly round with concentric rows of pointed teeth, like a lamprey's. Each stalk with a lot of these at the end, each mouth on a small tendril, so it can extend outward to latch onto prey. The movie shows them consuming the good wheat that's all around these deadly plants, and then, when there's no wheat left to eat, they pull themselves out of the ground and move off in search of additional prey!!!!!!

No one has ever accused me of having a dull imagination. . .

The king was bothered when he woke up. Who wouldn't be? But for some reason, unlike other nightmares, this time he couldn't shake a nagging feeling of menace that persisted even after he was awake. Somehow, he intuitively realized that these dream, bazaar though they were, nevertheless he felt that they were saying something important to him. But what?

No one could tell him, no matter what person he asked. What did these dreams mean? What did they portent? No one knew.

There were court magicians, soothsayers, fortune tellers,

astrologers and all manner of such hovering around the court of the Pharoah. Not one of them knew what the dreams were about. To be sure, many said to Pharoah, "Your majesty, these dreams mean ______, and there's nothing to worry about!" I'm quite sure Pharoah heard this at least a dozen times. But such interpretations did not ring true to him.

That's the way with dream interpretation. The final interpreter of the dream is the dreamer. Only the dreamer can truly say whether or not the interpretation rings true.

So, Pharaoh was frustrated because he went through all the known dream interpreters and despite their authority as 'dream interpreters', everything they told Pharoah simply did not feel right. Finally, though, his cupbearer remembered that young Hebrew in the dungeon from two years ago.

Then the chief cupbearer said to Pharaoh, "I remember my faults today. Once Pharaoh was angry with his servants, and put me and the chief baker in custody in the house of the captain of the guard. We dreamed on the same night, he and I, each having a dream with its own meaning. A young Hebrew was there with us, a servant of the captain of the guard. When we told him, he interpreted our dreams to us, giving an interpretation to each according to his dream. As he interpreted to us, so it turned out: I was restored to my office and the baker was hanged."---Genesis 41: 9-13

Why so long?

Don't know. Scripture is silent on this, as there is so much spiritual silence when we are in dark times. Why does God take so long to lead us to a better place? This is a mystery. One of the main truths of life, life as a follower of Jesus Christ, is stated by

the prophet Habakkuk and repeated (and expanded) by Paul is:
The just shall live by faith.---Habakkuk 2: 4 and Romans 1: 17

Change that word 'faith' to what it really means: trust. Faith in scripture carries the core meaning of to trust in God, that is, Jesus, both in the Hebrew stems and in the Greek. It's the same thing we mean when we look at our teenager, who is worried (as only a teen is worried) about what some friends or teammates might think or say about something our teen has done and our son, our daughter, is worried about whether or not he/she will be able to handle the consequences. We, the parent, look at our wonderful son, our wonderful daughter, and say, "You will. You can handle whatever happens. I have faith in you."

I have confidence in you, and I am and always will be loyal to you and to your best interests. I trust you.

Having faith in Jesus Christ, that is, trusting Jesus, means having confidence in Jesus that Jesus will be, consistently and always, who he has revealed himself to be (in the Gospels and the words about him in the rest of the New Testament). Rising out of such confidence is a deep loyalty to Jesus that stays with us throughout time. (This is my bottom-line summary of what I have discovered to be the most profound writing about faith, what it is and how it works, that I have ever read, namely H. Richard Niebuhr's *Faith on Earth An Inquiry into the Structure of Human Faith,* 1989)

We have faith that God is with us, no matter what. We trust God. That is to say, we are confident that the Holy Spirit, God himself present to us, is with us wherever we go, especially in suffering in this life. We are confident in this because we know, and know deeply, the story of Jesus Christ, of all that happened to him, all that he did and how God, Jesus's Father and, through Jesus, OUR Father, brought victory to Jesus when everything came, seemingly, crashing down onto Jesus' head, on the cross. It was God who raised Jesus from the dead, welcoming Jesus into the fullness of the kingdom first through the resurrection and then through the ascension. The contact with Jesus, God incarnate we say in faith, available to the disciples and those who followed him on earth, continues to be available to us so many years later through the Spirit. We are confident from what we have learned and experienced that the Spirit, the Holy Spirit, is Jesus himself, present to us in our lives today, and therefore not bound by the limitations of time and space.

God in Christ is with us. Always. We have confidence in this. We are loyal to this affirmation in how we live. We trust Jesus Christ our Lord and Savior. We have faith in Jesus Christ our Lord and Savior.

I went into all that to show that in the Bible having faith in Jesus is far more than giving intellectual assent to certain propositions about Jesus and God declared to be true. Such as Jesus is the Son of God, Jesus died for our sins, etc. To be sure we sometimes hear the phrases 'The faith of the church', or 'Defender of the faith'. Notice the direct article in the last phrase, 'the'. The faith. Not something interior within us, like trust, but something outside of us, an object. This means the 'set' of beliefs about Jesus articulated first in the Nicene Creed and somewhat later the Apostles' Creed. These are a series of intellectual assertions about Jesus that arose from controversy, conflict and confusion among Christians three hundred years (or more, in the case of The Apostles' Creed) after Jesus was crucified and rose from the dead. The phrase 'the faith' along with "having faith in Jesus" are quite often, especially among clergy and academic theologians, short phrases that encompasses all the intellectual assertions about Jesus contained within both of these ancient creeds.

I want readers of this little book to realize, if they did not already, that there are two basic meanings of 'faith', of 'having faith': (A) Faith as trust, as confidence in and loyalty to, and (B) faith as giving intellectual (i.e. cognitive) assent to certain assertions about Jesus as being true. At the risk of oversimplifying, we can say that A deals with the heart while B deals with the mind. All of us are prone to lean toward one or the other. Lean towards, not be. The real, gritty truth is that all those statements in the creeds, and everything the Apostle Paul and Mark and Matthew and Luke and John and Apollos wrote about Jesus emerged from their deep confidence in Jesus and their loyalty to Jesus, their deep trust in Jesus and how this trust changed their lives. A and B are not complete opposites, having nothing in common with one another. Rather, they are different points on a circle. Diametrically opposite from each other perhaps, but still, within the same circle, feeding into one another.

I could say a great deal more about 'faith', but I trust that now, when I speak of having faith in God or faith in Jesus, I am not referring so much to the 'head' aspects of faith but more to the heart aspects.

So, we have faith in God, in Christ our Lord, when we go into the dark times. It is this faith, this simple trust, that sustains us through such times. We learn to live one day at a time, living in hope, hope that we will make it through dark days and darker nights, and coming to the awareness that this hope comes from Christ's Spirit brushing against us. Because there is no hope left within us. It's been pressed out of us.

As we make our way through such times we battle our feelings of bitterness, of resentment. It's hard, for although we know we should let grudges go, it's almost impossible to shut off the pictures that play through our minds, pictures of what our so-called friends (maybe even our family members) said or did over and over. In such times we so wish we could shut such memories out, shut our memories off.

In our better moments we know that holding grudges, nurturing resentments is not good, that doing such things end up causing us trouble eventually. But when the time comes, and come it will, and we begin to move on, it just may be that our inner self is so twisted by bitterness and hurt that we carry a large portion of that dark place with us into the light.

There's a reason that stories of revenge are popular; always have been and always will be. All of us have experienced injustice in some way and there's that part of us that would relish seeing those who hurt us finally get what's coming to them. Probably the greatest such story comes from the prolific pen of the nineteenth century French writer Alexander Dumas, his *The Count of Monte Cristo.* Edmund Dantes is nineteen years old when he is set up and betrayed, being sent to prison when he had done nothing wrong. After several years of imprisonment, he is on the verge of committing suicide when an old priest bursts surprisingly into his cell, having mistakenly tunneled there trying to dig his way to freedom. The old man befriends Dantes teaching him many things, most especially about a great treasure he discovered and hid. When he dies Dantes takes his place in the burial sack (their version of a body bag) and escapes. He then learns who betrayed him and where they are. After retrieving the secret treasure, he then goes about planning and carrying out an elaborate revenge scheme on them all.

Like most nineteenth century French (and English!) novels it's long and has multiple characters and plot lines, for the original novel was published by Dumas (as did Dickens) over a number of months as a continuing serial in a magazine. It was to the authors financial advantage to keep the story going as long as possible, meaning more characters and more sub plots and sub-sub-plots.

Still, the novel, even now in the twenty-first century, sells. That's amazing! Plus, it's prompted many adaptations as movies and plays as well as giving the essential story to subsequent novels. My favorite among many is *The Stars My Destination* by Alfred Bester, which is the basic story of *The Count of Monte Cristo* retold as science fiction. Very good science fiction, I might add.

Even more recently, Netflix released its eight-episode adaptation of Jack Carr's   novel *The Terminal List.* It's a story of revenge with Chris Pratt playing navy seal commanding a seal team that is set up and wiped out, all but Pratt. After this establishment of the plot the rest of the episodes detail how this seal commander proceeds to learn who betrayed his team and takes them out. All of them. There is absolutely no mercy in this series, and it ends with Pratt quite literally sailing away into the sunset. The multiple executions Pratt commits apparently have no effect on him at all. Which, personally, I don't buy for a second.

The series was very popular on Netflix, less so among critics. What I roll over in my mind is the fact that this series was popular. Why? Couple of reasons, not least because Chris Pratt has the lead. Mr. Pratt is a very good actor, whose basic demeanor comes across as an Everyman, a common guy, very approachable and down-to-earth. I have no idea whether or not he is this way in real life, but he definitely comes across like this. Also, given this was the actor playing the lead, I and a whole lot of other people probably thought the series was going to be a roller-coaster ride of a thriller about how this regular, faithful, responsible guy gets back at those who betrayed him. Gets back at them. Meaning, exposing them, toppling them from power. Gives 'em what's coming to them. But that's not this story. This story turned out to be a very grim tale of revenge with no mercy for anyone. Which really bothered me. Most thriller movies are almost never this consistently grim and completely justice oriented, justice tempered by no mercy whatsoever.

This was popular? Maybe a lot of people were like me,

beginning the series intrigued by the three episodes and then watching the remaining to see just what happens to the villains and to the main character. Then, when we finish the final episode are disturbed at the way things played out.

Or maybe not.

Which REALLY gives me pause.

I do wonder just how many of us go through our dark times and emerge very twisted, very hurt, very angry. It's years before we calm down, if we ever do.

I want you to notice, then, how Joseph comes before Pharaoh. Remember who Pharaoh is: the highest authority in the land, the arbitrator of all grievances. Joseph could come before him and say things like "OH! Mighty Pharaoh! May you live forever! I thank you for pulling me out of that dark and gloomy place! I am so glad I can talk to someone who will listen to me and has the power to help me. Let me tell you about all that's happened to me, for I have thought of almost nothing else for two and a half years! And your cupbearer, he forgot about me! After I helped him to get out! He left me there, in the dark, after he promised to help me. Let me tell you how wronged I have been!!!!"

Pharaoh sent for Joseph, and he was hurriedly brought out of the dungeon. When he had shaved himself and changed his clothes, he came in before Pharaoh. And Pharaoh said to Joseph, "I have had a dream, and there is no one who can interpret it. I have heard it said of you that when you hear a dream you can interpret it."

Joseph answered Pharaoh, "It is not I; God will give Pharaoh a favorable answer."

Then Pharaoh said to Joseph, "In my dream I

was standing on the banks of the Nile; and seven cows, fat and sleek, came up out oof the Nile and fed in the reed grass. Then, seven other cows came up after them, poor, very ugly and thin. Never had I seen such ugly ones in all the land of Egypt.

"The thin and ugly cows ate up the first seven fat cows, but when they had eaten them no one would have known that they had done so, for they were still as ugly as before. Then I awoke.

"I fell asleep a second time and I saw in my dream seven ears of grain, full and good, growing on one stalk, and seven ears, withered, thin and blighted by the east wind, sprouting after them. And the thin ear swallowed up the seven good ears.

"But when I told it to the magicians there was no one who could explain it to me."

Then Joseph said to Pharaoh, "Pharaoh's dreams are one and the same; God has revealed to Pharaoh what He is about to do. The seven good cows are seven years, and the seven good ears are seven years; the dreams are one. The seven lean and ugly cows that came up after them are seven years, as are the seven empty ears blighted by the east wind. They are seven years of famine. It is as I told Pharaoh; God has shown to Pharaoh what He is about to do. There will come seven years of great plenty throughout all the land of Egypt. After them there will arise seven years of famine, and all the plenty will be forgotten in the land of Egypt; the

famine will consume the land. The plenty will no longer be known in the land because of the famine that will follow, for it will be very grievous. And the doubling of Pharaoh's dream means that the thing is fixed by God, and God will shortly bring it about.

"Now therefore let Pharaoh select a man who is discerning and wise, and set him over the land of Egypt. Let Pharaoh proceed to appoint overseers over the land and take one-fifth of the produce of the land of Egypt during the seven plenteous years. Let them gather all the food of these good years that are coming and lay up grain under the authority of Pharaoh for food in the cities, and let them keep it. That food shall be a reserve for the land against the seven years of famine that are to befall the land of Egypt, so that the land may not perish through the famine."---Genesis 41: 14-36

Even after interpreting the dreams and all that comes after, there is no mention in the biblical record of Joseph saying to Pharaoh, "Let me tell you how I've been wronged!"

In fact, judging from his later conversations with Pharaoh when his brothers come to Egypt later in the story, it seems as if Pharaoh had no idea as to Joseph being sold into slavery by his brothers. Also, nothing more is said about the chief cupbearer's failure to remember Joseph.

Joseph's heart, his inner self, his will, was turned not to the negative and reliving his darkness over and over, but to each new day, planning for the future. Joseph did not complain about what happened to him, nor did he mull over in his mind possibilities of taking revenge on his brothers. At least there's nothing of this in the story. If he did turn over in his mind his betrayals, his hurts, then he did not give in to dwelling on such things.

This can be extremely difficult for some of us because we have been hurt deeply by those whom we love, by life exploding on us. Such hurts can dominate our thinking. The problem is that we can shift almost imperceptibly into dwelling on these things so much that become bent, even soured on life. We cannot enjoy a sunset because viewing a beautiful sunset reminds us of past hurts, when we were with that person or persons, laughing, enjoying life, only shortly thereafter to turn on us. We cannot even enjoy an ice cream cone because the ice cream cone reminds us of that day when we were enjoying ice cream cones and he/she betrayed us.

Simple, everyday pleasures become tainted with hurt because we keep remembering, over and over and over and over and over and over the hurts done to us. Years have come and gone and we're still brooding on these hurts.

There was an older lady in one of the congregations I served who was rather brusque and terse with just about everybody. Most people had little to do with her because of this. Several people who knew her well told me that she was a 'real prickly pear'.

When I began work at a different church one of the first things I always did was to secure a list of the shut-ins, those members who can not now attend, usually because of health reasons. This lady was on this list, so I dutifully called on her to introduce myself as the new minister. She was polite to me, but it didn't take long for her negativity to kick in, as she complained about the state of her home, her health, and on and on. I do remember as I drove away thinking that I had definitely been told the truth about her: she WAS a prickly pear!

I called on the shut-ins once every month when I could, because there weren't that many. So, as the months rolled by and I visited her eventually we got to know each other a bit and became more comfortable with each other. She softened up a bit, but only a little bit! About eight or nine months into my tenure at the church, during one of my visits, she began to tell me of her son who, in her mind at least, had betrayed her. He had gone off and married a girl that she greatly disapproved of. The young woman was rather 'loose' in this older woman's eyes. She and the woman's son had done things together that were definitely wrong, but they had paid the price over time. Now they were happily married and had been so for several years. Yet this mother could not let go of her hurt from her son, years after the events, years after the punishments had been endured. She held onto her hurt feelings like Midas clutching his gold. It poisoned not just her relationship with her son and daughter-in-law, but these hurts prevented her from enjoying all of life that surrounded her. All she could talk about, over and over, was how bad things were, how mean people were, how folks could not be trusted. Everything was negative.

And then something interesting happened. Her son and daughter-in-law had a child, a little boy. At first, when the parent brought the baby over for her to see, the bitter woman would have nothing to do with the baby.

Until he became a toddler. And then the energy and innocence of a child began to work its spiritual magic. One day we were sitting at her little table in her kitchen talking and once more she was ruminating on her disappointment in her family when, suddenly, she paused and said slowly, "But it's really not fair to put all this onto that little boy, now, is it Reverend?"

I looked at her. "No," I said gently, "it's not." And we began to talk about letting go the stuff we keep inside and replay over and over. Slowly she began to let go of her hurts, her disappointments that had stayed inside of her for so long. Although I was called to another church not too many months later, on my last visit with her I could see that that terrible bitterness that had pinched her face, especially around her eyes, was gone. She looked a bit more relaxed, and definitely was in a better mood!

From Charles Dicken's Miss Havisham in *Great Expectations*, still wearing her bridal gown for years because her lover had abandoned her at the altar and she never got over it, to my older friend, all of us go through betrayals, misunderstandings, losses of temper that we have so much trouble forgetting; the time we got fired, the time we thought our friend had our back at work, only to discover anything but; the time our spouse asked to separate, and then going through the divorce. So many, many hurtful experiences. Going through them and the emerging out of them is a great spiritual struggle.

God gives us a great lesson in Joseph, for when he moved on in his life, he did not take this dark baggage with him. He remembered, oh yes indeed! As we will definitely see in the coming chapters. But he did not allow his memories, his past hurts, to overwhelm him or control him. He moved on and went into a very different place.

Notice this too: not only did he interpret Pharaoh's dreams through God's grace in giving him the skill to do so, but he also recommended a masterplan to cope with the upcoming famine.

When we move on, if we open ourselves to the new place in which we now find ourselves, we can realize that there are things to do in order to get through the day and work for future goals. When we bring our baggage with us, it's hard to look to the future when dragging past hurts with us.

Joseph offers us a great example: when we move on, then move! Deal with what's happening to you each day on its own merits, which are tricky enough. Heaven knows, Joseph and Pharaoh had their hands full with what they had to do each day for the next several years in order to be ready for what they knew would be coming at them.

The proposal pleased Pharaoh and all his servants. Pharoah said to his servants, "Can we find anyone else like this--one in whom is the spirit of God?" So, Pharaoh said to Joseph, "Since God has shown you all this, there is not one so discerning and wise as you. You shall be over my house, and all my people shall order themselves as you command; only with regard to the throne will I be greater than you"

And Pharaoh said to Joseph, "See, I have set you over all of the land of Egypt." Removing his signet ring from his hand, Pharaoh put it on Joseph's hand; he arrayed him in garments of fine linen and put a gold chain around his neck. He had him ride in the chariot of his second-in-command; and they cried out in front of him, "Bow the knee!" Thus, he set him over all of the land of Egypt.

Pharaoh gave Joseph the name Zaphenath-panetah; and he gave him Asenath daughter of Potiphera, priest of On, as his wife. Thus, Joseph gained authority over the land of Egypt. Joseph was thirty years old when he entered the service of Pharaoh king of Egypt. And joseph went out from the presence of Pharaoh, and went through all the land of Egypt.---Genesis 41: 37-46

By the way, did Joseph ask to be appointed Pharaoh's right-hand man? No. Even though he could have. He did not promote himself; he left this up to the authority over him, and up to God.

When you live for God, each day, trusting the Lord Jesus Christ to be with you and to help you, when you do your best to not allow painful, hurtful memories crowd around you and smother you, then your very character shines. Joseph was noted for his character; this means the way he lived, the way he carried himself, the way he worked with people. Pharaoh said he did not know anyone in Egypt as wise and discerning s Joseph.

Joseph was thirty years old when he waws elevated to serving the king and being overseer of all of the land of Egypt. Age does not necessarily mean maturity or immaturity. It's how you live your life that proclaims whether or not you're mature.

Thinking back over what the Bible says about Joseph's finally moving on, here's four things to consider.

1. During our waiting period in dark times we are called to trust God as we've never trusted God previously. And to do so without panicking. The temptation, always, is to flail our arms, complain, complain, complain. What we feel is that we're abandoned, perhaps even been betrayed by some close to us. We feel alone, isolated.

I do think that sometimes we believe that if we make enough noise in our life perhaps someone will notice us and rescue us. The truth is, God has not abandoned us, not matter how much we feel as if He has. The Bible along with so many Christians who have come through experiences teach us that God is still with us, even when we cannot feel his presence; that not only is God with us, helping us to keep on going, God will lead us out of our dark place to a place that is actually lighter. But, in God's time, not ours.

And here's something I've learned as well, through walking through my own dark times: it might get worse before it gets better. This happens more often than we want to admit. If it does, remember not to panic; trust the Lord, trust Jesus.

You WILL make it through. You really will.

2. Somewhere along the line, as we live each day, we are going to be presented with opportunities that require us to utilize skills and talents we have developed. Don't let these pass. Such opportunities may require us to go out of our way a bit. They may require us to get a bit of retooling to develop certain skills we innately possess. But opportunities will present themselves to us, and many times these opportunities are ways out of our dark places, as was Joseph's opportunity to do dream interpretation, first to the cupbearer and baker, then to Pharaoh. It may take a while but never let opportunities that utilize your personal skills and abilities pass you by, especially when you're living in tough times.

3. When you move on then leave behind what you need to leave behind. If you do not you risk sabotaging everything good that's happening to you, and eventually you'll land right back where you were, in a dark and lonely. The Confuser (my personal name for the devil, as well as the biblical term The Accuser) is listened to far too often. The Confuser does not want us to be healed and move on, oh no. He wants us to remember our hurts, all of them, remember them in detail, play them over and over in our minds so we stay hurt, we stay angry. Doing this puts up a big wall against the love of God coming into us. God, as shown us through Christ, wants us to be healed, wants us to move towards wholeness, wants us to experience real peace deep inside.

4. This may be quite unnecessary to name, but I'll take a chance on this because I believe we cannot say it too much: as we move on remember that always with us, bringing healing, bringing light into us, is our Lord Jesus Christ. Always. Always. Always.

So! If you have been raised with Christ, then seek the things that are above, where Christ is,

seated at the right hand of God. Set your minds on things that are above, not on things that are on earth, for you have died, and your life is hidden with Christ in God.---Colossians 3: 1-3

Our life is not just OUR life; our life is also embraced by Jesus Christ. Almost literally Jesus has taken us into himself, hugged us tightly, covering us completely with his love, his power, his strength, his forgiveness. We are, crazily enough, 'inside' Jesus. Jesus is all around us. Jesus is before us, behind us, above us, below us, wherever we go we are always within Jesus' presence.

This is what Paul is getting at when he writes about being raised with Christ. He's talking not just about when we die, he's talking about right now! In our life RIGHT NOW! Something happens in us, literally. We are somehow, someway, transformed, renewed, strengthened.

And because we are, we have the strength and power to focus our minds on good things, on wonderful things, on beautiful things all around us! Things that we almost literally could not see when we were in our dark place. Things like the amazing beauty of flowers, flowers in the grocery store in their small and large tubes and pots, glorious flowers of all colors and hues. Why have I not seen them before, we think, knowing that we did not see them because we were so caught up in the worries and fears that crept upon us out of our dark place, squeezing us to become worried and fearful about things that we end up so focused on getting what we needed for our kitchens and pantries that blinders became fastened onto our eyes and we cannot see the beauty around us in our lives. Such fears, such worries sap the very energy of life itself out of us, and we way too often are not aware this is happening to us; we are not aware of how much we have been missing.

But then, thanks be to God, as we move on, suddenly, one

day, we become aware of the flowers in the grocery store. . . And then we walk outside and see the flowers outside. . . holy moly. . .

It's when we are remade from the inside out by the Holy Spirit coming into us when we've been in the dark for so long, coming into us and leading us into fresh air, this is when we begin to see things we have not seen in a long, long while. Things of beauty. Beauty incarnate right before our eyes. I'm speaking of the beauty of mountains and rolling hills and incredible towering walls of stone, of hearing the wind, the only thing making a sound, brushing through the pines along the ridge we're hiking, of peoples' smiles, laughter, especially the smiles and laughter of children. Amazing, beautiful things! Things like hearing a Bach fugue in four voices played amazingly on a magnificent pipe organ; we hear the initial subject, then hear it again as it tags along behind the first statement, then comes the third time, then the fourth, and all four are dipping and weaving among one another, the subject rising up for air now here, now there, and we sit and shake our heads in amazement. How can Bach compose such a thing? Four separate strands of theme, each developing, each in perfect cohesion with the others, and Bach brings them all together in a powerful conclusion that feels so deeply right.

I'm talking about things like hearing Beethoven's 6th symphony or Mahler's Second or Mozart's *Magic Flute* or Verdi's *Otello* played and sung so well there are tears in your eyes at the conclusion. I'm talking about things like the incredible virtuosity and artistry of the players in an amazing blue grass group, or jazz ensemble. I'm talking about things like dancers moving through their numbers with a smoothness that a laughing dolphin zipping effortlessly thru ocean waves would envy and the principal dancers executing their solos and the final pas-de-deux so exquisitely your breath catches and you feel tears on your face.

Beauty.

In so, so many forms.

I kneel in absolute awe and adoration before God who created us in such a fashion so that we can recognize and appreciate beauty in so many ways. Animals cannot do this. Only human beings. And why did God do this? Recognizing and enjoying beauty does not add to the probability of the continuance of our species, to use a common biological reason proffered as an explanation for much of human behavior. Chipmunks and dogs and cats and horses and rabbits and lizards and bees have promulgated their species with no conception of beauty behind their behavior. None. Yet we human beings tear up when we hear a special song on the radio, because it's sung so. . . beautifully.

Why did God make us this way?

Because he loves us. He wants us to be able to experience and appreciate what is beautiful, for doing so leads us into joy. Real, honest-to-goodness, deep joy. It's part of what Jesus is getting at when he told his followers "I have come that you might have life and have it more abundantly." (John 10:10) Have it more abundantly. What does that mean, what is Jesus getting at?

Consider this. We sit in a theater and after two and a half to three hours sparked by occasional bursts of laughter, then rise to our feet applauding the actors who have led us through the amazing highs and lows of Shakespeare's *Midsummer Night's Dream,* our eyes watering a bit as not only the human lovers are reconciled but even Oberon and Titania, and even old Bottom is thanked by the king and queen. Why are we so moved? And the words that Shakespeare wrote, why do they reverberate within us so?

And, at the opposite end, why are we struck, so deeply struck, that tears are felt on our cheeks as we watch old King

Lear emotionally tortured by his oldest daughters, even though his foolishness invited this. Compounded with Gloucester's blinding, Lear's complete frustration, fury and break-down on the blasted heath makes us tense, sit up straighter in our seat, even leaning forward a bit, drawn into the scene by the skill of the actors we're watching, and then finally, when we think we can take no more, at the very end of the play, onto the stage shuffles poor, pitiful Lear carrying the dead body of his youngest daughter. And the words, the words. . . the flood of words that we speakers of English sit in awe of, their descriptive power, their almost uncanny ability to say things that resonate so deeply, these words. . . At the play's end inside ourselves we cry out "Oh GOD!!!!" and our feeling for Lear, for Cordelia, for Gloucester, for the play, is deep indeed.

Why are so moved?

For goodness' sake, it's just a story!!!!! It didn't really happen! If it didn't really happen, then it's not real, and if it's not real it doesn't mean anything. Right?

If it's not real, then why are most of us so drained after watching this particular play? And why do we shake our heads, marveling at such a work, such artistry? Why do we, amazingly, feel cleansed, as if something has washed our souls. What in the world can make us feel something like this? Not real? Of course it's real! It's real to our souls, to our deepest depths it speaks of deep truths, and so many of us say that it is beautiful.

It is beauty not of appearance, as in a beautiful woman, a beautiful man, as beauty is almost always defined in this our stunted, limited age of TV and internet adolescent pundits, but beauty in the sense of seeing a portrayal of the deepest truths of what it means to be a human being, whereby we say that such a portrayal, such a play, is beautiful. Only a writer so skilled that such a writer is called an artist can do such a thing. Instinctively we recognize such rareness, and therefore say that Shakespeare's plays are things of beauty, while so many plays simply do not justify giving them such a name.

It's when we've lost the ability to perceive beauty that life becomes very, very empty, very much a drudgery, and there is no joy, no real happiness to be found. It's only when, by God's grace, we begin to move away from such a place, and we begin to perceive snatches of beauty here and there, and then more and more, only then do we begin to realize just how terrible a place it was that we lived in.

Being able to perceive beauty all around us, especially in the people around us, is one of the most amazing gifts God gives to men and women. Life, the life of our soul is, quite literally, restored to us.

This is what God, Jesus Christ our Lord, does for us: He gives us back our life in all its depth and breadth. Jesus' energy, Jesus' power comes into us, because Jesus knows us, loves us, forgives us. Because he loves us this much, he will give us strength and power to let the past be the past, helping us to become open to new opportunities, open to new life stretching before us, open to life, with all its beauty.

This isn't a fairy tale.

This isn't a bed-time story.

This is actual fact.

This is truth.

Trust me on this.

Now,

Go out, and LIVE!!!!!!!!!!!!!!!!!!

JAMES R.M. YOUNG

The Story of Joseph
How God Works in Our Lives

CHAPTER FIVE

Facing Your Past

Joseph is now in charge of food production & storage in Egypt. He is a leader and a very important man.

Just as Joseph had predicted, interpreting Pharaoh's dreams, Egypt proceeds into 7 years of great plenty, great crops, which are then followed by the years of drought and famine. But it wasn't just in Egypt that the drought caused problems, it was all over the middle east. The countries surrounding Egypt were hit just as hard, including the place where Joseph came from, Palestine.

When Jacob learned that there was grain in Egypt, he said to his sons, "Why do you keep looking at one another? I have heard," he said, "that there is grain in Egypt; go down and buy grain for us there, so that we may live and not die."---Genesis 42:1-2

Food was getting scarce, for people and for their livestock. Things are starting to get serious; serious enough for Jacob to send his sons to Egypt and see if the stories about there being food in Egypt are true.

If so, they need to purchase what they can so the family will not starve to death.

Remember, though, none of them have the faintest idea of what has happened to Joseph. They believe he's dead.

So, ten of Joseph's brothers went down to buy grain in Egypt. But Jacob did not send Joseph's brother Benjamin with his brothers, for he feared that harm might come to him.---Genesis 42:3-4

Remember Benjamin? He's Jacob's youngest son, and Benjamin's mother was Rachel. Jacob loved Rachel especially, having labored in his father-in-law's employ for fourteen years before the cunning old man had permitted Jacob to marry Rachel.

It makes sense that the two boys she bore Jacob would have a special place in Jacob's heart, especially since Rachel had died giving birth to Benjamin.

Now, just who gave birth to whom can be a bit confusing, so I've prepared a little chart that lists the twelve sons of Jacob, from whom are derived the twelve tribes of Israel mentioned often in the rest of the Old Testament.

<u>The Sons of Jacob—thru 4 women</u>

Leah (older sister of Rachel) --Reuben; Simeon; Levi; Judah; Issachar; Zebulun.

Bilhah, Rachel's Maid/Servant---Dan; Naphtali.

Zilpah, Leah's Maid/Servant---Gad; Asher.

Rachel (younger sister of Leah) ---Joseph; Benjamin

I put the two sisters, Leah and Rachel, in bold because they are Jacob's legal and official wives. Yes, in those days of the patriarchs, polygamy was permitted.

What confuses us today are the other two mothers of sons, Bilhah and Zilpah. The first, Bilhah, is Rachel's maid; the other, Zilpah, is Leah's maid. According to the customs and mores of the day, the children born of the union of the head of the household with one of the servants is a legal one as far as the child being a legitimate heir to the father's estate. The son born of such a union has just much right to the estate after the father's death as any son born of one of the 'official' wives.

What happened was quite simple. Jacob, in love with Rachel (the younger sister) was tricked by the girls' father Laban, into marrying the oldest sister, Leah. By the customs of the middle east in those far -off days the oldest daughter was married first, plus the younger sister could not marry until the oldest daughter was married. This was the custom not only for the middle east back then but was true for European history as well. This tradition is what fuels the plot of one of Shakespeare's early (and thoroughly delightful) plays *The Taming of the Shrew.* The surprise in this story is Laban did not bring up any objections to Jacob marrying Rachel before Leah. That should have been a serious red flag to Jacob (and to Rachel). But, I suppose, they were too much in love to notice such things. But I suppose they were too much in love to notice such details.

The trick Laban pulled on Jacob was so simple it's almost comical. Because the custom in that day and age was for the bride to be brought to the groom with a veil over her face, and minimum words required by the bride until the wedding ceremony was over, it was simplicity itself for Laban simply to switch brides, putting Leah under the Bridal veil, and having Leah go through the ceremony with Jacob.

Remember, in those days women, especially young women, had nearly no say in who they married. Obviously, Leah knew that Jacob loved Rachel, not her, but she went along with her father. But why didn't Rachel say anything until it was all too late? Wasn't she at the wedding, somewhere? Maybe. Maybe not. . . And it all was probably done VERY quickly, at the very last second, substituting Leah for Rachel. Possibly some of Laban's most trusted servants simply absconded with Rachel as she was getting ready, and Leah put on her sisters' clothes and veil.

To give Leah the benefit of the doubt, she probably didn't want to go along with her father's scheme, I'd like to think that she loved her sister. She may have been attracted to Jacob, but to deliberately go along with her devious father into tricking Jacob into marrying her? This is film noir/femme fatale territory. It's possible; but I don't think it happened that way. I think it was a last second action with Laban forcing Leah into playing her part. To us today we immediately think, Laban may have forced her to take Rachel's place, but she could easily have lifted the veil and stopped the ceremony.

This is how much culture has changed. The individual, to us, is more important than family, and individual happiness trumps everything in our culture. Not back then. Loyalty to family, and to the head of the family, trumps everything. It was simply not on Leah's radar screen to stop the wedding ceremony, to go against what her father had specifically ordered her to do. And notice this: at no point in the text does Jacob blame Leah in any way. Not at all. Jacob gets it that in their culture Leah had no choice but to obey her father. It was all Laban's fault, and his alone.

So, when Jacob realized just who it was he had married and confronted his father-in-law, Laban calmly said to his now enraged son-in-law that it's the custom to have the older sister married first. If Jacob wanted to still marry the younger sister, he's more than welcomed to. . . provided he works for Laban for another seven years.

Which Jacob did.

Sigh. . . the course of true love never did run smooth.

Like I said, the scriptures are usually more interested in results, in what happened, rather than talking about people's feelings. So we know next to nothing about Jacob's feelings and his relationship with Leah, or, for that matter, with Rachel, once he marries her, seven years after he married her older sister.

Not to belabor the obvious, I do think it's safe to say that Jacob liked Leah enough to have not just one, but six sons by her, over the years. I say that because I do think that Jacob became very fond of Leah. Otherwise. . . .

But sisters will be sisters, and because Leah seemed to have no difficulty at all in getting pregnant, younger sister Rachel became rather exasperated, let's say.   And those of you who have sisters can understand what was going on quite well. Big sis was always better at some things than baby sis and loved to let baby sis know this. Which irritated baby sis to no end. But sometimes, she'd get back at older sis by being good at things older sis had trouble doing. Every parent of more than one child knows this see-saw very well.

I'm quite sure this went on between Leah and Rachel. But this, this getting pregnant, not once, but twice, and then three times. . . then four times!!!!!! Then (GASP!) FIVE!!!!!!!!!!!!! THIS was going WAY TOO FAR!

Rachel couldn't even conceive once?!!!! It was all so unfair!!!!!

So, if she, Rachel, could not get pregnant and give her beloved Jacob a son, then she'd do the next best thing: she'd give Jacob her maid, Bilhah, as a surrogate mother. Take that, Leah!!!

Well, two can play at that game.

Leah gave Jacob her maid, Zilpah, as a surrogate mother too.

Aren't families wonderful?????

(This whole story can be found in Genesis 29 and 30.)

Now, before I get back on track with the story of Joseph's brothers going to Egypt to buy food, let me take the liberty of, once more, pointing out the obvious. It is true that the bible does not get into

Jacob's relationship with Leah, his feelings about her, her feelings about him, in any in-depth way, which is frustrating to many of us (but has also offered fruitful ground for novelists). Nevertheless, the Bible does give a few hints about the dynamics in this ménage-a-trois, as in Genesis 30:14-15. In these short verses it's clear that the sisters apparently swung back and forth, being jealous of the other, depending on who was with Jacob at the time, and just who (and who's maid) was pregnant. I do think, though, that Leah was inevitably more jealous of Rachel because no matter what he would say to her, and no matter how many times she would become pregnant and give him another son, Leah had to know that Jacob still and always preferred her younger sister over her. That had to gnaw at her.

Now, ask yourself this question: what did these boys see growing up? What did they see when Jacob was around Leah and then around Rachel, not to mention Bilhah and Zilpah? How would Jacob treat the sons of Leah? of Bilhah? of Zilpah? How did these 'brothers' interact with one another? (And let's not forget that Leah, and probably the two maids, also gave birth to girls as well as all those boys. We're not sure how many, but based on the few references in the text, the boys had sisters.) Think about this, and about the favoritism shown by Jacob to Joseph.

When you really start to consider all the dynamics that had to have been going on in this family for decades, the wonder is not so much that Jacob favored Joseph as he did, but that this family didn't fly apart at the seams.

*　　　*　　　　*　　　　*

Let's begin this story of the brothers coming to Egypt and Joseph encountering them by asking ourselves just how old was Joseph when his brothers came to Egypt to buy food? We have to do a little bit of digging, but we can answer this question fairly closely.

Later on in the story (Genesis 41:46, to be exact) we read that: "Joseph was thirty years old when he entered the service of Pharaoh king of Egypt."

Ok, that gives us something definite to work with. He's thirty when he becomes Pharaoh's right-hand man.

There are seven years of plenty, according to Pharaoh's dream, so at the beginning of this cycle he's thirty, and then he's 37/38 when the drought & famine first begin.

The question at this point is just when did the brothers make their journey to Egypt? Was it during the first year of the drought, the second, the third? the fourth?

They come to Egypt at the beginning of the third year of the drought because Joseph says to his brothers, "The famine has been in the land these two years, and there are five more years in which there will be neither plowing nor harvest." (Genesis 45:6)

If Joseph was 37/38 when the famine began, then two years into it he is thirty-nine to forty years old.

I want you to think about something. When we graduate high school, most of us are around 17/18, right? Ever been to your 20th high school reunion? And you haven't seen these 'friends and acquaintances for 20 years? Whew! It's a shock, seeing these forty-year-old adults that if we met them on the street wouldn't make much of an impression at all. Just regular people.

But this group of forty-year-olds are not regular people, they were our high school classmates. The picture we have of them in our heads is not as a forty-year-old adult, but the sixteen, seventeen, eighteen year old teenager we remember from high school. The super athletic guys . . . well, a few are still in decent shape, but more now. . . well. . . you can tell that they have not been dieting for a while. . .

The thin, great-looking girls so many of the guys were in love with are now moms with hair a lot shorter (baby-hands love to grab mom's hair) and they're. . . and, like all of us at the reunion, none of us are shaped like we were when we were seventeen or eighteen years old.

And then, perhaps most surprising of all, the classmates who, when we last saw them, were simply not all that attractive, male or female, why, goodness gracious!!!! They're attractive now!!!!

Point: there's no way the brothers will recognize their skinny, seventeen-year-old, bratty brother who is now a grown, mature forty-year-old man who is in charge of all of Egypt! And carries himself with appropriate dignity for the office he holds.

Now Joseph was governor over the land; it was he who sold to all the people of the land. And Joseph's brothers came and bowed themselves before him with their faces to the ground. When Joseph saw his brothers, he recognized them, but he treated them like strangers and spoke

harshly to them. "Where do you come from?" he said. They said, "From the land of Canaan to buy food." Although Joseph had recognized his brothers, they did not recognize him. ---Genesis 42: 6-8

It seems that Joseph immediately recognized his brothers. Maybe. I think that at first Joseph did not recognize them, but when Reuben, the oldest, spoke, and said where they were from, that was what triggered Joseph's memory. I don't think he ever forgot the sound of his oldest brother's voice. That voice that told everyone what to do and how to do it. That voice that was always saying something like, "This is the way our father wants this done!" Joseph had heard that voice in those tones saying those things from the day he first drew breath. He never forgot it. I don't think any of us forget the voice of our oldest brother (or sister) telling us what to do. Remember also that Joseph would be using an interpreter. No Egyptian official would be likely to speak Hebrew. His brothers definitely did not speak Egyptian. So, while the interpreter was translating Joseph had a few seconds to look closely at these men from Canaan. Sure enough, he began to recognize them, each and every one of them.

Joseph addressed them using a rough, sharp tone of voice.

Joseph also remembered the dreams that he had dreamed about them. He said to them, "You are spies; you have come to see the nakedness of the land!"---Genesis 42: 9

What dreams? These dreams. "There we were, binding sheaves in the field. Suddenly, my sheaf rose and stood upright; then your sheaves gathered around it, and bowed down to my sheaf. . . Look, I have had another dream; the sun, the moon and eleven stars were bowing down to me." (in chapter 37)

These dreams have just come true before Joseph's eyes: "And Joseph's brothers came and bowed themselves before him with their faces to the ground." (Verse 6, above) It's an interesting touch, this little note about Joseph remembering the dreams. What it implies is that this whole story of Joseph is exploring the amazing truth that there is more going on here than just the story of Joseph and his brothers. There is a power greater than the brothers at work here. In fact, there is a power greater than Joseph himself at work here.

Ok, sure, it's in the bible, so it's about God looking after Joseph, yes, we get that.

If you thought that, or something similar when you read the above sentences, that's fine. But if you did, then it's quite possible that this is your own way of dodging something that seems to be too amazing to be true, namely that there is a power, greater than you, at work in your life.

May not seem like it. In fact, the direct opposite may appear to be the truth, that everything in your life is just one thing after another. No particular pattern. You've done well at some things, not so good at others. But it was you who was engaged, your decisions not some power or whatever looking after you. If there was such a power, many of us think, then that power could have been doing a better job.

I have a feeling that Joseph didn't think he was being looked after very well either. I mean, think about it: sold by his brothers into slavery, condemned to a dungeon for years for something he didn't do, and so on.

But God was with him. God had always been with him. God was looking after him. God was working through him to help others in a way that he had no idea of until he saw his brothers. Then he remembered his dreams, which he now realized were a foretelling of the future.

God is looking after you too. Even though it may not seem like it.

God has you close to him and wants to help you face what you need to face, shoulder what you need to shoulder, and live, live deeply, even joyously. I'll have a lot more to say about this as we continue, but for now, please notice something: Joseph, in living honestly, in hope, in faithfulness to what he knew to be right, was finally lifted from his dark dungeon, and God also was able to bless so many other people through Joseph.

Remembering these dreams started Joseph to thinking about his journey from being a spoiled teen to eventually grow into an Egyptian leader helping a whole lot of people survive. It wasn't so much God was looking after just him, that was definitely the case, God was; but the greater mystery is that in God's hands, Joseph's survival, linked with his doing what was right and true, resulted in hundreds, thousands of people being saved from starvation.

One of the great mysteries of life and of faith is that God always works in us to bring good in some way, not just to ourselves, but to others also.

We touch others' lives all the time, and we're

unaware of it, like George Bailey in the movie *It's a Wonderful Life.* Take George out of the picture and so many lives were affected, even to the point of the whole town changing.

We, all of us, are far more of a blessing to others than we will ever know. And this is all part of God's hand in our lives.

(And, conversely, when we do not do what is true, when we do not live the way God wants us to live, we hurt many more people than we ever dreamed of. This is why each and every one of us is so important to God, to OUR Heavenly Father.) Note the plural reference.

There is a mysterious and quite real power at work in all of our lives, in our ups and downs, our good and bad, our great times, our tragic times, a power that is always lightly tugging at us, touching us ever so softly. A power for good, for hope.

You may not believe this, but trust me, it's true. Very, very true.

Joseph said to them, "You are spies; you have come to see the nakedness of the land." They said to him, "No, my Lord; your servants have come to buy food. We are all sons of one man; we are honest men; your servants have never been spies." But Joseph said to them, "No! You have come to see the nakedness of the land!" They said, "We, your servants, are twelve brothers, the sons of a certain man in the land of Canaan; the youngest, however is now with our father, and one is no more."

But it is just as I have said to you; you are spies! Here is how you shall be tested; as Pharaoh lives, you shall not leave this place unless your youngest brother comes here! Let one of you go and bring your brother, while the rest of you remain in prison, in order that your words may be tested, whether there is truth in you; or else, as Pharaoh lives, surely you are spies."

And Joseph put them all together in prison for three days.---Genesis 42: 9-17

Whew. . . what's going on here?

Spies? Could be. Egypt had enemies all around. These 'brothers' could very well be sent to get the lay of the land for an attack by some chieftain, some petty ruler, to get at the food storage. So while they were in prison, Joseph could send out a recon force to check the northern border to see if there was any threat building up.

But what's really going on is that Joseph needs time to think. What is he going to do?

He probably never thought he'd ever see his brothers again and seeing them shocked him.

He'd dealt with his past by leaving it in the past. Now it's standing in front of him.

So. What does he do?

Does he get back at his brothers for treating him the way they did? Does he physically hurt them? Whip them? I'm sure he thought about this. But you know something? That was a long time ago. . . that was then, this is now. The truth is Joseph thought he'd never hear Hebrew spoken again. . . that accent, that way of speaking that sent him zipping back to his childhood and teen years before everything crashed. I'm sure that while they were in prison, Joseph would stop by and look at them, perhaps from some secret opening where he could see them, but they could not see him. Reuben the oldest, the one who was bossy, but who also loved him. . . heh . . . he still combed his hair the way he did. . . but it's now really gray!!!!!!

And Simeon and Judah. No one could make everyone laugh like Judah, and was he ever protective of his youngest sister, Dinah. . . And that made him think of the one he was closest to, his baby brother, his only full blood brother. He and Benjamin were the only children Rachel had birthed. Oh! How he wanted to see Benjamin!!!!!

But did they even miss me? Joseph had to have thought this. Did they hate me that much? Did they just forget about me? And Dad. . . Oh, Lord, Dad. . . how is he?

For three days Joseph struggled, and his brothers struggled too. He had to have seen them looking more and more haggard and distressed.

Joseph, at his core, in spite of everything that had been done to him, was a kind man. And they were his brothers, so:

On the third day Joseph said to them, "Do this and you will live, for I fear God: if you are honest men, let one of your brothers stay here where you are imprisoned. The rest of you shall go and carry grain for the famine of your households, and bring your

youngest brother to me. Thus your words will be verified, and you shall not die." And they agreed to do so.---Genesis 42:18-20

Okay, well and good. One brother is kept as a hostage and the others freed. To free the one who has to stay is simple: bring Benjamin back. That will solve everything, free the brother who had to remain and prove to the Egyptian leader that they were not spies.

Sounds like a plan.

They said to one another, "Alas, we are paying the penalty for what we did to our brother; we saw his anguish when he pleaded with us, but we would not listen. That is why this anguish has come upon us."

Then Reuben answered them, "Did I not tell you not to wrong the boy? But you would not listen. So now there comes a reckoning for his blood."

They did not know that Joseph understood them, since he spoke with them through an interpreter.
---Genesis 42:21-23

The story has this exchange occurring in front of this audience with Joseph. The brothers were speaking Hebrew, which they assumed no one around them could understand. But Joseph could and did.

Here's the point, and it's HUGEt: What they did

to their brother has HAUNTED THEM FOR TWENTY YEARS!!!!!!! They all remembered Joseph's cries from the pit begging his brothers to get him out. But they sat around the edge, pulled out their lamb and mustard sandwiches, and calmly ate their lunch. They sold him. They looked at their little brother as he was bound and chained and put into a cart with other slaves. He looked at his brothers, tears streaming down his face. And they calmly watched him be taken away.

I think what finally got to them was Joseph's pleading, loudly at first, but as he was bound and placed in a holding cart, his crying got softer and softer. . . please. . . please. . .don't let them take me. . .I'm your brother. . . please. . .

His tear-streaked face and his final, soft whimperings have become a tape inside all of their heads that would not stop, just playing over and over and over. . .

Every day. Every night.

For twenty years.

When we do something that we know is wrong, something that really goes against what's really deep in us, we never, ever forget this. Never.

It all may get quiet in our souls for a while, but then, when we get stressed out, or when things start to go wrong for us, or when we are especially tired, once again, bubbling up like noxious gas from some thick tar pit, comes these memories. Memories of what we said, our tone of voice, what we did, how those we hurt looked at us. We can tamp such things down again and again. But life seems to be structured in such a way that we eventually meet the part of ourselves that we have tried to hide from or tried to say was simply not part of us. Usually this is when our lives start coming apart because our own denials, our own attempts to hide or deny our dark side no longer work.

The affair is discovered.

We get in a wreck when we're high or drunk and someone is severely injured.

We lose our job because of what we've done, or what we've been doing.

Our spouse says, "I can't deal with this anymore, I've had it!" and walks out, with the kids.

Our past finally catches up with us. We cannot deny it any longer. We cannot avoid any longer what we've done, what we've said.

Facing the truth about ourselves always hurts. This is precisely what the brothers are experiencing here in the dungeon. Joseph went through this in his own dark place, the slave pen and the dungeon, facing his own obnoxiousness over time, coming to grips with the reasons his brothers did what they did to him.

Now his brothers are having to face their own past, and their guilt about what they have done to their brother comes tumbling out. They can no longer avoid talking about it, facing it.

Carl Jung, when he was a senior citizen, once said that just about every psychosis he had dealt with in his practice was, he believed, rooted in the fact that most of his patients refused to bear the normal and necessary pain of living.

What apt phrase he said, 'the necessary pain of

living.' Life hurts, sometimes a lot. A whole lot. And, at some point in our lives, we all have to bear the pain of facing who we really are, and what we have done that we are not proud of, perhaps something that we are even very ashamed of. This pain of facing our own ugliness, our own incredible selfishness, our own cruelty, our own meanness and what it's done, this may very well be one of the hardest, most personally painful things we ever do. Yet this is the true and only path to healing, to experiencing real peace.

Joseph turned away from them and wept; then he returned and spoke to them. And he picked out Simeon and had him bound before their eyes. Joseph then gave orders to fill their bags with grain, to return every man's money to his sack, and to give them provisions for their journey. This was done for them.---Genesis 42:24-25

Joseph's orders to his brothers are fascinating because he is actually duplicating what happened to him: leave one of the brothers in Egypt and end up with a pile of money to be brought home with them.

What will they do? Will they forget Simeon, just like they forgot Joseph, once they discover that they have money and food? Oh sure, they've expressed regret, admitted their guilt; but talk is cheap. Will they leave a brother, AGAIN, and take money home AGAIN, and forget all about that brother. . . AGAIN?

They loaded their donkeys with their grain and departed. When one of them

opened his sack to give his donkey fodder at the lodging place, he saw his money at the top of the sack. He said to his brothers, "My money has been put back; here it is in my sack!" At this they lost heart and turned trembling to one another, saying, "What is this that God has done to us?"
---Genesis 42:26-28

Indeed, what IS God doing?

At some point, as we face our darkness inside, our past, and realize we MUST change somehow, someway, because we cannot continue with the way things are, at some point, the pull of the past, the pull of the old way becomes very, very strong:

--the old way is familiar; it worked for a while, maybe it will work again.

--that other person is so beguiling, so attractive, maybe even has a bit of money.

-- we tell ourselves again, just like we always have, I can stop drinking on my own, I know I've messed up bad, but I can stop. . . I'm not really a drunk.

Let's be very, very honest here: the new way that comes about because we've faced our past, admitted what we needed to admit, the new path that grows from this, is strange, because it's unfamiliar, it's new to us. And truth be told, it actually scares us. We've been doing the old for so long we've sort of buried any other way. We can't remember what it's like to be sober for two straight weeks, much less two months. We've played games with the accounts for so long that it scares the daylights out of us not to have all that financial cushion. She called me on the phone, or he texted me. . . just wanted to talk. . . I was just listening. . . and then we, well, we did some things we shouldn't have.

What is God doing to us, asked the brothers and that is exactly right: what is God doing to us, making us face what we've had to face. And now. . . what?

The truth is, God is leading us, just as he was leading Joseph's brothers, into real healing, into real hope, into real peace. But to get to what is real, we have to go through a period of pain. We hurt inside, in our souls, because what we're doing and what we're experiencing is different from the way it's been for so long. It's strange to us.

We are now entering a time in our life that quite possibly may be the most frightening time we have ever experienced. There's no other word for it. Everything we've gotten used to, even though so much was destructive, nevertheless, we were familiar with it. At least we knew what to expect, of those around us, of our own bodies. But this new place we find ourselves. . . maybe we were there once, but it was years ago. . . maybe even several decades. . . and it's scary now. Really, really scary.

I think that this is part of what the apostle Paul was getting at when he talked about working out your own salvation with fear and trembling: "Work out your own salvation with fear and trembling; for it is God who is at work in you, enabling you both TO WILL and TO WORK for His good pleasure." (Philippians 2:12-13) It is the Spirit of Christ himself, working in the depths of our consciousness, helping us to live differently. It is not just our own will power; there is a power deep within us that we have never accessed until we faced what we had to face and turned to God in Jesus Christ.

Paul summarizes this experience magnificently in his letter to his friends at Ephesus.

But now in Christ Jesus you who once were far off have been brought near by the blood of Christ. He is our peace. In his flesh he has made both groups into one and has broken down the dividing wall, the hostility between us. Jesus has abolished the law with its commandments and ordinances, so that He might create in Himself one new humanity in place of the two, thus making peace. It is Christ who, through his death on the cross, who reconciles both groups to God in one body, putting to death all mutual hostility.

Jesus came and proclaimed peace to all of you were far off, and he also proclaimed peace to all of you who were near. It is through Christ that both groups have access in one Spirit to the father. So then you all are no longer strangers and aliens, but you are citizens with the saints and members of the household of God, built upon the foundation of the apostles and prophets, with Christ Jesus himself the cornerstone. In Christ Jesus the whole structure is joined together and grows into a living and holy temple in the Lord in whom you also are united together spiritually into a dwelling place for God.---

Ephesians 2: 13-21

This may not be the easiest passage in Paul's letters to understand, but the idea is actually quite simple. Paul is talking about the Jews and gentiles coming together through Christ. And we can extend this basic idea so that it indicates how God in Christ works within us. Paul speaks of the one new man, Christ himself, who reconciles those who have been so torn, so at odds with one another, so hostile to one another that they were unable to come together in any way.

This is true for each one of us. Think of it this way: the part of us that is guilty and the part of us that is condemning ourselves, we, the good and the bad parts of us, are brought together in a healing that transcends the ages. By Jesus.

Jesus went through the darkness, in Gethsemane and the agony of the Cross so that he might bring to us, in our darkness, in our time when we're at the end of our rope, forgiveness, healing. He gives us the power to actually experience hope plus real strength to move forward into something new, something right, something that actually works in our lives.

We are no longer strangers, wanderers through life, but we are members of the household of God. This new, strange, somewhat frightening place where we are now is built upon the prophets and apostles, Jesus Christ himself being the chief cornerstone.

In other words, everything about our new life, strange and scary though it might appear at first, is where we need to be. Everything in us is actually joined together rightly for the first time! Now we are actually growing into something new and different. That is to say, each one of us is becoming a new and different person, a better person, through Jesus.

This is happening because you are now, actually and truly, the dwelling place of God himself in his spirit in you. He is transforming you! The power of God in Christ is working in you! Trust that power, trust the Lord's work in you, and live new!

The Story of Joseph

How God Works in Our Lives

CHAPTER SIX

<u>Being Negative</u>

You know, it just seems that it's a whole lot easier to be negative than positive.

I mean, think about it.

The day starts to unravel not after lunch but within ten minutes after we get started. We're moving things around the house and accidentally jostle a table knocking to the floor one of our favorite knick-knacks where it shatters into a thousand pieces. Our friend at work leans over our cubicle staring at us and says very seriously 'I need to talk to you.' We get a much lower grade on that test than we thought we would.

On and on. When we've had a bad day, watch out.

And, truth be told, although we all can be negative, some of us seem to be naturally inclined that way. We've always been so. The gas gauge is not half full it's half empty, and those who think otherwise are not being realistic.

If we tend to be this way, we also tend to take some pride in our inclination to be realistic. We are not the ones who blue-sky things, that's for dreamers and poets; you know, the ones who tend to fail at life because they aren't realistic. They don't plan for the way things, especially people, really are, and so their business goes under, their sales come up short constantly. Only hard-nosed realism works in the business world, in academia (contrary to what so many think), in school, in fact, in all of life.

I think Jacob was like this, the way a great many guys are (and not a few women, too!) The bible shifts our attention to Jacob, to his reaction to what his sons tell him when they return from Egypt.

When they came to their father Jacob in the land of Canaan, they told him all that had happened to them, saying, "The man, the lord of the land, spoke harshly to us, and charged us with spying on the land. But we said to him, 'We are honest men, sons of our father; one is no more, and the youngest is now with our father in the land of Canaan.'

"Then the man, the lord of the land, said to us, 'By this I shall know that you are honest men; leave one of your brothers with me, take grain for the famine of your households, and go your way. Bring your youngest brother to me, and I shall know that you are not spies, but honest men. Then I will release your brother to you, and you may trade in the land.'"

As they were emptying their sacks, there in each one's sack was his bag of money. When they and their father saw their bundles of money, they were dismayed.

And their father Jacob said to them, "I am the one you have bereaved of children; Joseph is no more, and Simeon is no more and now you would take Benjamin?!!! All this has happened to me!"---Genesis 42:29-36

What's the first thing Jacob does when he hears about one son being held hostage, and that to free this son, the youngest needs to go to Egypt? Why, he blames his sons for all of this mess!!!! Says it's all their fault that Simeon is now in Egypt. They had nothing to do with Simeon being kept in Egypt, it was totally out of their control. But Jacob is on a roll: "You have bereft me of my children! Joseph is no more and Simeon is no more!"

Well, that's true of Joseph, but Jacob does not know that; remember, he thinks a wild animal attacked Joseph. Of course, you'd think the brothers should have been protecting their younger brother, but still. . . In other words, it's the brother's fault.

For many of us, when our anxiety is high, and our stress is great, all too often we attack those closest to us. We accuse them of contributing to what is making us so upset, so anxious. Whether or not it's their fault is, when we're in such a state, beside the point. There's something inside of us that just lashes out, attacking those around us, blaming them for what has happened.

Our most convenient target is our family, our spouse and our children. They're the ones who take the brunt of our attacks. Perhaps they said something that triggered the outburst, and we tear into them, criticizing what they're doing, blaming them for little things that irritate.

The truth is that we're actually mad at something that happened with people at work, a supervisor got on our case or a deal is in jeopardy, or we got a notice from the bank about the money we thought would come through but now we know it's not. Or we've received that report from the doctor that we were dreading, and it's bad.

The fact is, we're scared. We're afraid that things are going to come apart, perhaps a bit, perhaps a lot. Out of such fear, we are prompted to attack and blame those closest to us. Our outburst is way out of proportion to what prompted it. That's because there's other things going on in our consciousness than what we SAY we're upset about.

A whole lot of us are built so that when we're afraid we become fairly aggressive. This is true of men and women. When afraid, for whatever reason, we rip and tear into those closest to us when they had little, if anything, to do with what's stressing us out. We become unreasonable. We become stubborn, seriously stubborn, and no one can talk sense into us. Because they're all addressing what they think is the problem, what we may even have said is the problem, but which is NOT the REAL problem.

Acting this way is destructive. It's like pouring acid on our ties to the ones we love most. Acting this way eats at these ties until these prime relationships that form the very foundation of our lives are actually in danger of being severed.

Jacob has lost Joseph. He's lost Rachel. Now Benjamin is threatened. No way is he going to permit his youngest to leave home. No way. He's not losing another child.

Question: who said anything about losing Benjamin? Who said one word about Benjamin being threatened? No one. This is Jacob thinking this in his own mind. The brothers know that Benjamin is not threatened, at least there didn't seem to be a threat. All that 'the man, the lord of Egypt desired, was to make sure they weren't spies. This would become clear when they produced Benjamin; he would be the proof that they were telling the truth, that they were not spies. There's no threat to Benjamin, and there won't be any threat to Simeon either if Benjamin comes back with them.

This is the real situation presented by the brothers to their dad. Jacob, however, is too stressed and too fearful to think clearly and logically. He's in full fight or flight mode, as Reuben finds out.

Then Reuben said to his father, "You may kill my sons if I do not bring him back to you. Put

him in my hands and I will bring him back to you." But Jacob said, "My son shall not go down with you, for his brother is dead and he alone is left. If harm should come to him on the journey that you are to make, you would bring down my gray hairs with sorrow to Sheol."--- Genesis 42:37-38

There's no reasoning with the old man; he's got his mind made up and nothing's going to change it. And logic has nothing to do with this.

Did you pick up on what he said about Joseph being dead? Joseph is no more, and if Benjamin goes to Egypt, then he will be gone too, and Jacob can't stand that because Benjamin is the only one left.

Excuse me? Benjamin is the only one left?

I thought he had twelve sons, Joseph being thought dead, so eleven.

What's this 'he alone is left'?

Jacob is thinking about Rachel, the woman he loved more than Leah. Rachel died giving birth to Benjamin, and this baby is now a young man, barely twenty, perhaps twenty-one, no more than twenty-two. He had to have been a toddler when Joseph was sold into slavery, twenty some years ago, because the Bible consistently refers to Benjamin as 'boy' or 'lad'.

Jacob is still, in a real sense, mourning the loss of Rachel, because what made this loss bearable was her two boys. But one was lost, and the other is now threatened, and everything that Jacob cherished about Rachel and Joseph, is about to be taken from him. Or so he thinks.

Men and women like Jacob tend to a negative view of things because they see things as they actually are, what is really and truly "there" in front of them, not what they hope to see or what they want to see. Such people have a great deal of difficulty believing in the reality of something they cannot see, touch, taste or smell. If they can't see it, or logically 'see' it (as in a budget/income), then it's not real. If they cannot touch it, it doesn't really exist.

For Benjamin to be away where Jacob cannot see him leads Jacob to give in to his deep-seated fear of losing Benjamin. It's almost like he's saying "I know you boys say you'll look after Benjamin and protect him and bring him back, but the truth is, once he's gone, he's gone. He's not here. I cannot see him. I cannot touch him. Therefore, for all practical purposes, he has ceased to exist."

I think this is how the old man is also thinking of Simeon. Simeon did not come back, he's not here, so he's "gone", period.

Perhaps you agree with Jacob. I can understand his fearing to loose Benjamin, given that he has lost Rachel and Joseph. But understanding and respecting a fear does not mean letting that fear control your thinking and your decision making. That's what Jacob, though, is doing. He's letting his fear control him, letting his fear twist his thinking, letting his fear shape how he perceives things.

He is afraid of losing Benjamin, but he is even more afraid of. . . what? What is driving all the energy that makes Jacob refuse to let Benjamin go? I think it's his fear of losing all contact with what helped him maintain his relationship with Rachel. In other words, he's afraid of losing his love for Rachel.

Joseph helped him because when he looked at Joseph Jacob could 'see' Rachel; at least his memory would be nudged into bringing up comforting memories of the good times he had with just Rachel, Joseph. But Joseph is gone and has been gone twenty years. Benjamin was all he had left that helped him remember and maintain contact within his memory, his consciousness, with Rachel and, for that matter, Joseph too .

For those who are very centered in what is actually before them, real, concrete, tangible objects associated with loved ones are extremely important. Most people like this find it difficult to simply think about the loved ones; holding or touching something that is closely associated with the loved one helps, helps a great deal. Thus, those who are naturally oriented this way put high value on such objects, particularly pieces of jewelry, necklaces, rings, watches, clothing, and most especially persons (usually children) who are closely linked to the loved ones. So, if Jacob lost Benjamin he feared that Rachel would become fainter and fainter in his memory, his consciousness of her, that his awareness of her would actually become thinner and thinner until she was no longer there with him in his mind because that real human being who served as a direct link to Rachel is no longer there. If he could not see that link, touch that link, then his contact with Rachel would disappear as well.

Recognizing that we, all of us, place high value on objects associated with loved ones, especially when these loved ones are no longer around, it's easy to see that sometimes we can put way more value on such objects than perhaps we should. And, when we start thinking about all of this, we know that these things, this ring, this necklace, this watch, this coat, these are things; they are not our loved one who is gone. We know this, we know this well. It's just that when these precious things are taken from us, it hurts, it hurts a lot. Somehow, some way we feel threatened when this happens, we feel a deep fear. What tied us to our loved one is now, because of theft, or fire, or water, or our own carelessness, now it's missing, and somehow this diminishes our sense of this loved ones.

When such things happen, when our valued objects are, for whatever reason, taken from us, we are challenged to remember what we know deep inside: this thing, these things, are not that special person. Losing the object does not do away with our memories, nor does it damage the love we had for the beloved, in spite of what our fears are. We can still remember their face, their touch, their scent, their hug. It's still very much registered in us. It's easier to bring such things to mind via holding the object, but we can still do this. Might have to work a bit at this, but we can still remember them in all the ways that are so important.

In our best, most lucid moments we know this. The problem is that when we are afraid, and especially when we fear losing a precious object or person that links us to one gone, such clear thinking goes out the window. We focus on the objects like a person who is drowning, gasping for breath as panic overtakes, trying with all our might to grab a life preserver that's just out of reach. That's when these precious things become a matter of life and death to us.

The other thing we do is get amazingly stubborn about all this. When we're in fear mode, fight or flight mode, and we make a decision about something, then by all that's holy we stick to it. Even if it's not a good decision!

Think about what we're doing here: we've decided in fear, we maintain our decision in fear, and from within this fear that covers us we're afraid to change our minds because of. . . because of. . . what? What will happen if we change our minds? THE WORLD WILL COME TO AN END!!!!!

Really?

I put it that way so that the next time you discover yourself behaving this way, ask yourself this question, what will happen if I change my mind, and then answer with the above, the world will come to an end. Hopefully you will at least crack a smile at yourself, and that will be the one pull that starts to loosen that hard knot inside of us that would not give an inch. (It's really amazing how humor can help us sometimes when we get stuck). Of course, the world will not come to an end, but we just might have to face a painful truth that our stubbornness has dodged. Like Jacob dodging the truth that sooner or later his family will need more food, and the only food available is in

Egypt. Meaning he's going to have to let Benjamin go with his brothers when they go back to buy more food.

As a result of Jacob's fear that led to him being so stubborn, Simeon stayed in jail a long time. Finally, Jacob comes around, but not until he is forced to. It's just like us so many times: if I ignore this problem, maybe it will go away. Or, thinking about all this hurts too much, so I won't think about it anymore. I've decided and that's that.

Until their food began to run out.

Now the famine was severe in the land. And when they had eaten up the grain that they had brought from Egypt their father said to them, "Go again, buy us a little more food."

But Judah said to Jacob, "The man solemnly warned us, saying, 'You shall not see my face unless your brother is with you.' If you will send our brother with us, we will go down and buy you food, but if you will not send him, we will not go down, for the man said to us, 'You shall not see my face, unless your brother is with you.'

Jacob said, "Why did you treat me so badly as to tell the man that you had another brother?"

They replied, "The man questioned us carefully about ourselves and our kindred, saying, 'Is your father still alive? Have you another brother?' What we told him was in answer to these questions. Could we in any way know that he would say, 'Bring your brother down?'

Then Judah said to his father Jacob, "Send the boy with me, and let us be on our way, so that we

may live and not die—you and we and also our little ones. I myself will be surety for him; you can hold me accountable for him. If I do not bring him back to you and set him before you, then let me bear the blame forever. If we had not delayed, we would now have return twice."--Genesis 43:1-10

I find it interesting that it's Judah who speaks to Jacob. Guess who it was that had the bright idea to sell Joseph into slavery? Judah.

To his credit Judah has apparently faced his own guilt somewhat and is ready to meet the consequences of his actions. Remember, all of the brothers hid the notion that their harsh reception in Egypt, with Simeon being kept there, was because of what they had done to Joseph twenty-some odd years ago. If Judah now admits his guilt, then for him to say here what he does, that he will be the one to be responsible for bringing Benjamin back safely, he will bear the blame if anything happens, this also means that he is taking responsibility for what he did to Joseph all those many years ago.

For Jacob, as for all of us at different times in our lives, we get boxed in, seemingly with no way to go save for one particular way forward: the intervention's choices to us, the rehab center or some extremely dire consequences; the divorce is finally finalized; the friendship for many years is ended. We have no food, everyone said to Jacob. This is the only possible choice. It's this or die.

Then their father Israel said to them, "If it must be so, then do this: take some of the choice fruits of the land in your bags and carry them down as a present to the man—a little balm and a little honey, gum, resin, pistachio nuts, and almonds. Take double the money with you. Carry back with

**you the money that was returned in the top of your sacks; perhaps it was an oversight. Take your brother also, and be on your way again to the man; may God Almighty (El Shaddai) grant you mercy before the man, so that he may send back your other brother and Benjamin. As for me, if I am bereaved of my children, I am bereaved." So the men took the present, and they took double the money with them, as well as Benjamin. Then they went on their way down to Egypt, and stood before Joseph.   ---
Genesis 43:11-15**

What a heart-breaking prayer. It's the prayer said by every parent when they discover something is wrong with their child and there are serious consequences ahead. It's the prayer said by every couple when the marriage is in serious trouble. If I must loose what is most precious to me, if this really has to happen, then I will do this with my eyes open, facing this directly.

Jacob was defeated. Jacob was beaten to the ground. Jacob was completely pessimistic about the future, totally broken in spirit. Life's circumstances have finally forced him to face the truth: in order to survive, not just him, but the whole family, his sons and daughters-in-law and all his grandchildren, for all of them to survive, Benjamin has to go to Egypt.

Facing the truth is the real first step in moving from the darkness, from the pit, from the endless cycles of hurt and destruction, into something better.

We all have to remember one of the great truths of life: God builds on truth. God cannot build on what is false.

And God does build. God always hears us when we cry such prayers. The Psalmist says a broken and contrite heart, O God, Thou wilt not despise . . . Create a clean heart in me, O God, and renew a right spirit within me. (Psalm 51)

God knows everything about us. God is sovereign over our lives, over our children's lives, over our parent's lives. God really is in charge, not us, no matter what the circumstances may be.

To be sure, we have the freedom to make bad choices and we must suffer the consequences of bad choices. But when we, in faith, turn to God and ask his help, and we have done our best to obey him in our lives, then this is living faith, and our heavenly Father will be with us. He will help us to face painful truths about ourselves, about our children, about our spouse... The Lord knows us, knows all about us, and still loves us with a love that passes all understanding.

It's all too easy to forget that God loves us and is with us when we pass through the deep waters of life. But He does, and He is with us, helping us to structure our lives when we obey him in ways that eventually lead us into light.

Just like He does with Jacob and Jacob's sons. But they could not see this light at the time, and neither can we when we're hurting. But the light is there because God is there. And although Jacob could not know it at the time, this was the turning point for him and his entire family into being restored as a family.

He thought it was the final straw in the complete dissolution of his family. It wasn't. It was the first step into being restored as a family. The whole family, for Jacob, for Joseph, for Reuben, for Benjamin, for Judah, for all of them. The whole family. This is a story of family systems theory millennia before there was any such concept, such is the wisdom of God.

Let me lift up some things for us to remember from this story.

First, if we have a tendency to perceive things in a negative way, admit this. Admit it to yourself. This is very important because those of us who have this tendency are prone to throw blame around fairly quickly rather than leap to admitting fault quickly. We say things like, "This is your fault! You didn't do what I told you to do! Nobody does things around here but me! If you would have listened to me, none of this would have happened."

Careful!

You may be right, but there's even odds that you're wrong. The better, more effective, more loving way is to be prudent. Don't be so quick to blame. Make your tongue be still for once.

Remember too, that those of us who tend to do this also, when really stressed, tend to catastrophize. By that I mean we exaggerate the problem. For example, we come home, and there's a few dirty dishes on the kitchen counter. It upsets us because we had asked the kids to stick them in the dishwasher. But, if we tend to the negative, and on top of this, we're really stressed, out of our mouth comes something like, "I told you to clean the kitchen!!! The whole kitchen's wreck, and the least you could do is help out around here, but no, you had to ignore me. You always ignore me!!! I'm the only one around here who ever cleans anything up!"

The whole kitchen wasn't a mess; just a couple of plates and silverware left out of the dishwasher. The kids don't' always ignore you, just this one time. They've done everything else you asked, but got busy doing something else and let the kitchen stuff go. And no, you're not, and never have been, the only one who cleans up.

Do you see what I'm talking about? Out of stress we perceive not a little problem but a huge one, and this perception adds to our stress. It's an extremely vicious cycle that goes on and on in us because we're not perceiving things correctly.

So, if you have a tendency to be negative, admit this to yourself, and watch yourself!

Second, remember that the Lord works through our mess-ups and failures just as he does through our successes. The last things we tend to perceive when things go wrong is God working for good through such happenings. We tend to think that God is judging us, abandoning us, teaching us a lesson, punishing us.

But God's judgments always are judgments to salvation, never strictly and only punitive.

God works through consequences for our welfare in the long run. He is always with us, especially in hard times and, most acutely in precisely those time when things are bleakest.

Third, we need to be careful about blaming. I mentioned being prudent, and that's a very good word, for it simply means to be careful and to watch and before making a decision.

What I want to remind all of us is that frequently blaming others will diminish prayer. We have trouble praying honestly when we're blaming others because we don't want to face the truth deep inside. When we're doing this, we're actually praying a lie, asking for God's help to be strong in the face of other's weakness or their inability to do what we believe they ought to. When the truth is that all that is happening is actually God's way of trying to help us to perceive the greater truth that what is happening is partially (and sometimes completely, though this is rare) our fault.

It's only when we stop blaming, stop complaining, that we can begin to perceive the truth. All that's happening to us may very well be God's way of leading us to see some painful truth about ourselves that we need to see. We need to be open about this, even if it makes us terribly afraid, but this is one way that God acts upon us to help us to grow into discipleship.

Lastly, and this is especially for guys, I want you all to notice something. Did you pick up on how the boys were trying to get Jacob to see the truth, but he would not because he was afraid, and at the same time, very prideful?

I control things! I protect this family! You boys couldn't protect Joseph and you cannot protect Simeon, and you sure can't protect Benjamin! I'm the one who can!

We guys often engage in a strange mixture of fear and pride being behind what we say and do. Fear of what's happening to our spouse, to our relationship, our marriage; fear of what's happening to our children. Yet pride in our ability to handle tough things at work, tough things even at home.

The problem is that these two emotions are like adding a minus one and a positive one. They cancel each other. The result is zero. That is, paralysis in our will.

We do not move. We stay right where we are. No decision. Put off making a decision. We decide not to decide.

If you're in such a place, then remember, the Lord Jesus knows our fear and our pride; he knows our anxiety and our stress.

Give these over to him and in return he will give you his yoke:

Jesus said, "Come to me all you that are weary and are carrying heavy burdens, and I will give you rest. Take my yoke upon you and learn from me, for I am gentle and humble in heart, and you will find rest for your souls. For my yoke is easy, and my burden light."---Matthew 11:28-29

In Jesus' day a yoke was a big, wooden harness that had leather loops attached to the bottom. The farmer slipped these leather loops over the ox's neck. A long leather strip attached to the yoke was held by the farmer. This was how he controlled the movement of the powerful animal. Similar to the way a bridle is for a horse, but different. Instead of the ox wandering away the animal's powerful strength was focused, directed to the real task at hand, turning the mill wheel, or pulling the plow, or wagon.

Jesus' point is obvious: too many times we find ourselves

wearing the wrong yoke, doing things that hurt instead of help, giving in to pulls in the wrong direction way too many times. Who's in charge of us? Are we really, deliberately hurting ourselves like this, over and over? To put this into today's language, who's jerking my chain?

We put on Christ, and notice that this is a deliberate choice; we are never forced, and it's very much like putting on clothes, clothes that we need so that we can face the harsh weather that we have to deal with. With Christ, we are able, slowly, oh so slowly, to perceive some light. With Christ we become able to let other people, especially spouse and children, into our lives in new and deeper ways. With Christ we can perceive the truth about ourselves more easily and more in-depth, because we come to realize that Jesus knew all this stuff about us, and was still there for us. In fact, amazingly, we come to realize that Christ was able to see all this stuff in himself too! So he can definitely help us to deal with our own destructive tendencies and habits.

The Story of Joseph
How God Works

in Our Lives

CHAPTER SEVEN

Prudence

So the men took the present, and they took double the money with them, as well as Benjamin. Then they went on their way down to Egypt and stood before Joseph.

When Joseph saw Benjamin with them, he said to the steward of his house, "Bring the men into the house, and slaughter an animal and make ready, for the men are to dine with me at noon." The man did as Joseph said, and brought the men to Joseph's house.---Genesis 43:15-17

For the moment Joseph is still reluctant to disclose his true identity to his brothers. I'm quite sure that his stomach had some butterflies when he was told that "the men from Canaan have returned." He had probably thought long and hard in his mind what he would do when they returned. IF they returned.

And so, he makes a great meal for them! But he does not yet reveal himself to his brothers; not just yet. There's still some thinking, still some reflecting that Joseph wants to do about these brothers who caused him so much hurt and pain.

Now the men were afraid because they were brought to Joseph's house, and they said, "It is because of the money, replaced in our sacks the first time, that we have been brought in, so that he may have an opportunity to fall upon us, to make slaves of us and take our donkeys."

So they went up to the steward of Joseph's house and spoke with him at the entrance to the house. They said, "Oh, my lord, we came down the first time to buy food; and when we came to the lodging place we opened our sacks, and there was each one's money in the top of his sack, our money in full weight. So we have brought it back with us. Moreover we have brought down with us additional money to buy food. We do not know who put our money in our sacks.---Genesis 43: 18-22O

Talk about being defensive! They were scared out of their minds! We're going be killed! Or maybe even worse, forced into slavery here in Egypt! All sorts of disasters flow into their minds from their imaginations. That's precisely what we do when we're confronted with an unknown situation: our imagination begins to create all sorts of terrors. Sometimes we can push ourselves into a high state of anxiety simply by anticipating all sorts of terrors, disasters and how many ways things can go wrong. It's always good to try and anticipate things to a certain extent so we can be prepared to take appropriate action or make a good decision. But for a lot of us, our imaginations can spin out of control.

Joseph's steward said to the men, "Rest assured, do not be afraid; your God and the God of your father must have put treasure in your sacks for you; I received your money." Then he brought Simeon out to them.

When the steward had brought the men into Joseph's house, and given them water, and they had washed their feet, and when he had given their donkeys fodder, they made the present ready for Joseph's coming at noon, for they had heard that they would dine there.

When Joseph came home they brought him the present that they had carried into the house and bowed to the ground before him. He inquired about their welfare, and said, "Is your father well, the old man of whom you spoke? Is he still alive?" And they bowed their heads and did obeisance.---Genesis 43: 23-28

In the bible, in the Hebrew Masoretic text that is the original language version that we have, the steward's first word is "Shalom!" He speaks a Hebrew word to these Hebrew men, a word ordinarily translated as 'peace be with you.'

The committee that prepared the New Revised Standard Version concluded that a better English phrase would be 'rest assured'. Perhaps. They were trying to convey the core meaning of that word 'shalom', usually translated as 'peace'. In this case 'shalom' conveys a sense of reassurance from the steward to Joseph's brothers that they did not need to be afraid of Joseph, that no harm would come to them. It is an interesting detail, having the steward first say this particular Hebrew to the brothers because, based on the brothers' anxiety I do not think that they expected the first word said to them in this situation would be their basic word for 'be at peace, there is no conflict between any of us here'. But, there it was; it was what the steward said. And I'm sure that their mouths may have opened a bit in puzzlement. What did he say? Did he say, shalom? To US? HIM?

WHY? What's going on here?

Joseph comes home for the mid-day meal, which for him is going to be the best Thanksgiving Day Dinner ever! Thanksgiving? Yes, because for most of us Americans, Thanksgiving Day is the one day in the year that so many of us try to get home to celebrate. Why? Because the whole family will be there, or as close as we can come to our whole family. It's the one time in the year (other than for funerals) that we as a family try to come together for a meal and be with one another more than thirty minutes. There's something about sitting around the dinner table (or, on the couch and every chair in the house, depending on how many were able to come) and seeing members of the family, members that we see usually only at Thanksgiving. Sometimes members of the family that we have not seen for years come to the feast, and that makes it even more special.

Joseph's 'mask' starts to slip just a little bit. He asks sincere questions about their welfare and especially their father's welfare. The brothers have to be perplexed. Just what in the world is going on here? Why does this Egyptian question us so closely about our family?

The narrator definitely likes this irony, with Joseph being the great Egyptian leader, and the brothers bowing and scraping before him. Just how often have they bowed before him. . . ?

Then he looked up and saw his brother Benjamin, his mother's son, and said, "Is this your youngest brother, of whom you spoke to me? God be gracious to you my son!"---Genesis 43:29

Joseph's gaze settle son his little brother Benjamin. Benjamin. . . who was barely a toddler when Joseph was sold into slavery. Benjamin, whom he had diapered, had given a bath to more than once. Benjamin, whom he has baby-sat, keeping him safe from the cattle, and out of the way of the busy adults all over the living area. Benjamin, little, baby Benjy. . . how he had gotten exasperated at him. . . gotten so frustrated at him. . . and how he had loved him. Oh, how Joseph had missed Benjamin!

And now, here he was. . . only not the toddler that Joseph saw in his mind. This was a strapping young man.   And he looked remarkably like. . . himself!!!! But, there was so much of Mom in him. . . his eyes were definitely Mom's eyes. . . but that mouth. . . and the way he looked at his brothers and at him, Joseph. . . .that was Pop to the core. . . . OH!!!! How did he get to be so big? How did he grow up so fast!!!!!

And then Joseph had to have bowed his head. . . it wasn't fast. . . it was twenty years. . . .Oh my God. . .

twenty years!!!!!

With that, Joseph hurried out, because he was overcome with affection for his brother, and he was about to weep. So he went into a private room and wept there.--- Genesis 43:30

Joseph allows himself to weep. In private, though; not in front of his brothers. That comes later.

Joseph opened himself up to the flood that was surging up from his soul. He allowed his grief, his hurt, his joy, all to come surging up.

He let himself be alive to this moment. He didn't shut himself off; he didn't push his emotions way down deep. He was mature enough to realize that sometimes it's a great gift to be reconnected with those whom you love, and it's also a great gift to feel deeply.

God gave us tears for a reason; sometimes we feel things so deeply that neither words nor expressions suffice. Tears can speak, speak eloquently of deep joy, deep sadness, and even deeply felt empathy.

There's something to be said for weeping in private. We are opening ourselves to things very deep inside of us, and it does make us quite vulnerable. We feel very exposed. It's appropriate to want to be by ourselves.

For some of us, though, we may be known for weeping, weeping in public over various things. If so, it may be good to rethink this, for when people see us weep, most naturally become sympathetic to our vulnerability. Those who weep a lot in public may be using this as a means of controlling those around them, trying to get them to be more sympathetic to us. That is, tears can become a way to manipulate others. And that is not good.

Then Joseph washed his face and came out; and, controlling himself, he said "Serve the meal." And they served him by himself and them by themselves, and the Egyptians who ate with him by themselves, because the Egyptians could not eat with the Hebrews, for that is an abomination to the Egyptians.

When they were seated before him, the first-born according to his birthright and the youngest according to his youth, the men looked at one another in amazement. Portions were taken to them from Joseph's table, but Benjamin's portion was five times as much as any of theirs.

So, they drank and were merry with him.---Genesis 43:31-34

Once Joseph had himself under control he returned to the room, but he did not reveal himself to his brothers. Not yet!

The feast commenced with the brothers at one table and the Egyptians at another, for it was forbidden by Egyptian custom for Egyptians to eat at the same table as foreigners.

Joseph does have a rich sense of humor. He deliberately informs the steward of who sits where, so that the oldest is in first position, and then the next in line, and so on until Benjamin. To make the joke even richer, Joseph quietly informs the servers to give the youngest Hebrew far more food than the others.

So, there they were, Reuben first, then Simeon, then Levi, then Judah, and so on down the line, in perfect birth order, to Benjamin.

Don't you know the brothers looked at each and asked, "How in the world did he know this? How did he know who was first born, then second and so on. . . all the way to Benjamin??!!!"

How indeed.

And then, to give the youngest far more, which completely flips the accepted way of things with the oldest getting so much, the second born some, and so forth and so on. Of course, this isn't true of meal portions, usually of inheritance; but the brothers had to have gotten a kick out of just how much this Egyptian leader appeared to be taken with their baby brother! Joseph had to have enjoyed the looks of incredulity on his brothers' faces. He was enjoying himself, and his little jokes hurt no one.

The text says that they ate and drank a long time. Even after this great feasting Joseph did not reveal to them who he was. Joseph waited. I'm sure he probably rehearsed in his mind all the things he wanted to say and to ask his brothers. But he made himself wait.

This had to have been hard, this waiting. The implication is that he wanted to talk with them some more on an informal basis, to explore just who they were now that they were all older.

In these stories about Joseph I have been trying to pull several things for us to think about that I believe are prompted by the text. But for this story, or rather this part of the story, I have only one thing for us to consider: the discipline of making ourselves wait. Of being prudent. Of not reacting.

This is so important to remember when we are in the process of moving on, of getting on with our lives, of facing having to make adjustments and decisions. Because we are moving into unknown or new areas of our life, the temptation is always to do what Joseph's brothers did at the beginning of this little episode: let your imagination go. Let it run wild with fears and anxieties: what's going to happen? I've been laid off! How will I pay the mortgage, the car payment, etc. etc.? The door clicks and our spouse is gone. . . now what? What do I do? What's going to happen to me? To the kids?

The fear we experience sucks the very breath out of us.

And it's precisely in such circumstances that the very best thing we can do is to pause. To think things through. To go through options, possibilities, but not in our own mind, because if you're like me, our imagination can highjack this thought process, and come up not with good options, but how many ways disasters will come upon us. I recommend doing such reflection with a trusted friend. A friend that we trust in such times is very much like Joseph's steward who said to the fear-struck brothers, 'Shalom!', peace be with you. You will be all right. You can deal with this. Let's think this through.

In such prudential waiting and reflecting, we can go over options, possibilities, such as taking or not taking the new job opportunity, marry him/her or not marry him/her, purchase that property or not, make the move out of the neighborhood, out of the area, or not. The Lord may indeed be wanting us to proceed in new directions, but it is always appropriate before making such a major decision to pause, to wait, to reflect, to be prudent and not just react.

Also, it's when we are waiting and reflecting that there's something else that Joseph did which is very much part of this whole process, namely allowing our real feelings about things to come to consciousness. It's probably most helpful to do this with a spouse or trusted friend.

We need to be able to perceive what is before us as it actually is before we move forward in making major decisions. Our tendency, all of us, is to have our perceptions skewed through our feelings. This is why it's crucial to let our feelings come to the fore and talk things over with someone who knows us, has our best interest at heart, and is not personally involved. Such a trusted person can usually perceive where we're not seeing things accurately.

In Joseph's case he was engaged in the process of trying to perceive the truth of his brothers: had they changed? Were they the same? Did they feel any guilt for what they had done to him? Joseph needed to know, and he needed to slow his own feelings down a bit, which is, I firmly believe, why he did not reveal himself immediately to his brothers.

The great lesson here is that when we do slow ourselves down, when we do pull back, when we do pause, when we do allow the practice of being prudent to operate, then we are working to make ourselves more open to perceiving clearly and objectively what it is that is facing us. We are better able to perceive the truth and better able to perceive how we may be avoiding the truth.

Some years ago I was working with a young couple, doing pre-marital counseling with them. As was my custom, after the initial meeting, I met with each separately and then met with them together so I could then share what I had picked up on their relationship. An important question I always asked was having them tell me where they wanted their marriage to be like their parents' marriage and where they wanted it to be different. The young man said, "For many years my dad really liked to go deer hunting in the fall. He loved it! He was gone almost a week. And my mom, well, she fixed his food for him to take, helped him to stock up, encouraged him to go and have a great time. Then, when he came back, she had a great meal waiting on him, and fussed over him when he came back. Man! That's really love! I want my marriage to be just like that!"

The young woman said, "When I was growing up Daddy always went off deer hunting for nearly a week in the fall, right at Thanksgiving! I hated that! So did my mom! We couldn't stand him getting ready and talking about it. But he was gone when it was so busy, our, meaning my mom and me, getting ready for the holiday. And he wasn't there, right when we really could have used his help! Then, when he came back he expected my mother to fix him a special meal, and if she didn't, he'd pout! Good grief!!!! I can't stand that! My husband better not EVER want to do something like that!"

Well. And no, I'm not making this up. Their expectations of one another actually were this extreme. We had some interesting discussions! My point is that these young people had been dating for nearly eight months. Of course, hunting had come up in conversations, and they been over to each other's families for meals and visits. But because they were "in love" with other, both pushed aside unpleasant expectations and behaviors. They knew that to talk about this was upsetting, and neither wanted to upset each other, or their relationship.

The truth, as we all know, is that these mutually contradictory expectations were going to come out and collide eventually. It was so much better for this couple to be able to explore their expectations in a far less anxious situation, namely before deer season began.

My question to all of us, no less to myself is to what extent are we skewing what we're looking at? To what extent are we avoiding things that we need to consider?

Pausing, taking the time to reflect, to pray, is God's way of helping us to pay attention to what's going on, to look at our lives, look deep. What is really going on with us? Is it right to move forward into life the way I was thinking I should; or is there another path? Am I really seeing things honestly, seeing her honestly, seeing him honestly, seeing the situation honestly? We may be pushing these questions aside because we get to whirling so fast that our life becomes a series of reactions: reacting to this guy, to that girl, to this situation at work, to that situation at school, to what we're told is going on in church, to what my husband or my wife said or did.

My concern is that, as I know so well from my own life, when we are simply reacting to things we are not grounded, we are not centered. That is why it's so crucial to take the time to pray, to reflect first within ourselves and then to a trusted friend, to listen, to be prudent.

The Story of Joseph
How God Works in Our Lives

CHAPTER EIGHT

I AM JOSEPH!

Things are starting to build to a climax. Joseph is really going to put his brothers to the test. He had to have thought out this whole thing quite carefully. After all, just how could he discover his brothers' real thoughts about him, how they felt about what they did to him, and have they really changed? He had heard their remorse while he kept them confined the last time they had come to Egypt. But that was then, and this is now.

The plan Joseph comes up with is rather ingenious in its simplicity. As the brothers had placed Joseph into danger years ago, so now he will, seemingly, put the youngest brother, Benjamin, into similar danger.

Joseph commanded the steward of his house, "Fill the men's sacks with food, as much as they can carry, and put each man's money in the top of his sack. Put my cup, the silver cup, in the top of the sack of the youngest, with his money for the grain." And he did as Joseph told him.---Genesis 44: 1-2

Ok, once again it's the brothers' money being put into their sacks. But, in addition to the money Joseph commands his steward to put his silver cup with the money. This is his divining cup, the cup through which he's supposed to tell the future, to be able to see far beyond what normal eyesight can see, to see at a distance.

Really? Seriously? Well, take this with a huge grain of salt.

Pharaoh was considered to be divine by the Egyptians, and so his first officer or prime minister should also have some sort of special power by virtue of being so close to Pharaoh. Archologists have discovered evidence that some distinctive Egyptians would take a special cup or chalice, fill it with an uncommon liquid (i.e. not water or wine), then place certain objects to float on the liquid. The Egyptian would then "interpret" or "read" the patterns the floating objects made, and thus see into the future or at a distance.

Since Joseph was the Prime Minister he would be expected to perform this custom. In addition, given that his father-in-law was an Egyptian priest (see Genesis 41: 45), he probably had studied the method with the older man and could make a good show of it when he had to. There is no evidence anywhere in the scriptures that Joseph believed in such methods of foretelling the future. The very fact that Joseph takes this particular cup and uses it in the way he did for this charade reveals just how little he thought of the cup. It was useful for his purposes, and this is probably how Joseph practiced divination, i.e. not putting one once of belief in it, but making a show of it because it was expected of him.

So, the special, silver, divining cup is put into one of the sacks, and Joseph bids farewell to his brothers.

As soon as the morning was light, the men were sent away with their donkeys. When they had gone only a short distance from the city, Joseph said to his steward, "Go, follow after the men, and when you overtake them, say to them, 'Why have you stolen my silver cup? Is it not from this that my lord drinks? Does he not indeed use it for divination? You have done wrong in doing this.'"

When the steward overtook them, he repeated these words to them. The brothers said to him, "Why does my lord speak such words as these? Far be it from your servants that they should do such a thing! Look, the money that we found at the top of our sacks, we brought back to you from the land of Canaan; why then would we steal silver or gold from your lord's house? Should it be found with any one of your servants, let him die; moreover the rest of us will become my lord's slaves."---Genesis 44:3-9

Big talk.

Of course they firmly believe the cup is not with any of them, so they can afford to talk big. "If it's found among any of us, then that person who had it, dies!!!! And. . . and. . . and the rest of us, we'll be your slaves forever!!!"

Whew. . . if they only knew. . . but they really thought the cup was not with them.

Joseph's steward, who had probably been coached by Joseph on how to handle this, simply stares at the brothers. Then he says,

"Even so, in accordance with your words, let it be: he with whom it is found shall become my slave, but the rest of you shall go free."   ---Genesis 44:3-10

There it is, the same situation that Joseph was in twenty years ago: a Hebrew cast into slavery. The one who is to be a slave forever is to be taken away, the rest of the brothers are to go back home. Just like it happened twenty years ago. To make this more poignant, the one to be cast into slavery is the one, remaining son of Rachel, Benjamin. He, like his brother, is destined to go into slavery. That's the plan Joseph has set up here. The question is, what will the brothers do when everyone discovers that the cup is in Benjamin's sack? Will they abandon Benjamin to go into slavery in Egypt? Just like they did with his brother Joseph? Or will they do something else? That's what Joseph wants to find out.

Then each one quickly lowered his sack to the ground, and each opened his sack. Joseph's steward searched, beginning with the eldest and ending with the youngest; and the cup was found in Benjamin's sack.

At this they tore their clothes.

Then, each one loaded his donkey and they returned to the city.

Judah and his brothers came to Joseph's house while he was still there, and they fell

**to the ground
before him.---Genesis 44:11-15**

Well, how about that? They DIDN'T abandon Benjamin! They all came with Benjamin back to Egypt!

If Joseph was surprised at this turn of events, he doesn't let on. He starts to act out being a tough guy:

Joseph said to them, "What deed is this that you have done? Do you not know that one such as I can practice divination?" (Oh, he's laying it on thick, he is!)

And Judah said, "What can we say to my lord? What can we speak? How can we clear ourselves? God has found out the guilt of your servants; here we are then, my lord's slaves, both we and also the one in whose possession the cup has been found."---Genesis 44:15-16

You'd think that seeing his brothers trooping back to stand before him, heads bowed, and then falling down before him in guilt, would be enough for Joseph to cut the charade. But not yet.

Perhaps because it was Judah who starts to speak, Joseph pauses just a bit. Remember, it was Judah who came up with the idea to sell Joseph to the caravan headed to Egypt. It was Judah who was the most blatant betrayer. It was Judah who hurt Joseph the most. It may be that looking straight at Judah, and Judah looking straight back at Joseph, that Joseph went ahead with the charade a bit more, actually making things more edgy, more menacing.

Joseph said to Judah and his brothers, "Far be it from me that I should do so. Only the one in whose possession the cup was found shall be my slave. The rest of you may go back to your father in peace."---Genesis 44: 17

There is absolute silence in the room.

People are barely breathing. Joseph is absolutely still, staring into Judah's face. Judah stares back, not moving. No one moves.

Then, Judah drops his eyes, hangs his head, and then looks over his shoulder at his brothers. They look back at him. Last of all, Judah looks at Reuben, his older brother, the brother who had wanted to go back to the cistern and pull Joseph out. Reuben looks at his brother Judah . . . and then drops his head. He knows what Judah has to do, what he has said he would do if things came to this point. Reuben knows that this is the last time he will see his brother Judah. . . because Judah had made a very specific promise to their father. And Reuben saw in Judah's eyes that this time, THIS time, he would do the right thing.

Judah lets out a huge sigh, raises his head, squares his shoulders, and looks straight at Joseph.

Judah took a few steps forward, coming close to Joseph, so that he could speak quietly to him, directly to Joseph.

"Oh my lord," said Judah in a low voice, "let your servant please speak a word in my lord's ears, and do not be angry with your

servant; for you are like Pharaoh himself. My lord asked his servants, saying 'Have you a father or a brother?'

"And we said to my lord, 'We have a father, an old man and a young brother, the child of his old age. His brother is dead; he alone is left of his mother's children and his father loves him.' Then you said to our servants, 'Bring him down to me so that I may set my eyes on him.' We said to my lord, 'The boy cannot leave his father, for if he should leave his father, his father would die.' Then you said to your servants, 'Unless your youngest brother comes down with you, you shall see my face no more.'

"When we went back to your servant, my father, we told him the words of my lord. And when our father said, 'Go again, buy us a little food', we said, 'we cannot go down. Only if our youngest brother goes with us, will we go down; for we cannot see the man's face unless our youngest brother is with us.

"Then your servant, my father, said to us, 'You know that my wife bore me two sons; one left me, and I said, Surely he has been torn to pieces; and I have never seen him since. If you take this one also from me, and harm comes to him, you will bring down my gray hairs in sorrow to Sheol.'

"Now therefore, when I come to your servant my father and the boy is not with us, then, as his life is bound up in the boy's life, he will die, and your servants will bring down the gray hairs of your servant, our father, with sorrow to Sheol. For I, Judah, your servant, became surety for the boy to my father, saying, 'If I do not bring him back to you, then I will bear the blame in the sight of my father all of my life.'

"Now therefore, please let your servant, I, Judah, son of Jacob, son of Isaac, son of Abraham, remain as a slave to my lord in place of the boy; and let the boy go back to with his brothers.

"For how can I go back to my father if the boy is not with me? I fear to see the suffering that would come upon my father."---Genesis 44:18-34

And there it was, what Joseph had desperately been hoping for: his brothers HAD changed; they WERE willing to make a huge sacrifice so that the youngest, the one remaining son of Rachel, the one son who was so precious to their father, that they were willing to do what they had to so that old Jacob would not be hurt again. In fact, the one who had hurt Jacob so terribly all those years ago, the one who callously disregarded his brother, now is ready to give his life for his brother.

One of the definitions of maturity is to be able to perceive life in a realistic way from another's point of view. When you're young, it's very difficult to do this. Now, though, Joseph's brothers are older. They probably have children of their own. They know what it's like to suffer as a parent. They do not want to add any more suffering to their elderly father.

But, more importantly, they, and especially Judah, are willing to accept the consequences of their actions. They had done wrong years ago; they know this, they know it well, for it has haunted them ever since. In some mysterious way the things that were happening to them now seemed somehow, someway, to embody the justice they believed they deserved. The text is silent about such feelings being expressed by the brothers, but I do think it's highly probable that they felt this way. Lord knows, if I would have been in their shoes I would have. Without batting an eye, Judah, the one who was most responsible for Joseph's fate, offers himself up to the same fate he helped his brother to twenty years previously.

It's almost more than Joseph can stand.

Then Joseph could no longer control himself before all those who stood by him, and he cried out, "Send everyone away from me!" So no one stayed with him when Joseph made himself known to his brothers. And he wept so loudly that the Egyptians heard it, and the household of Pharaoh heard it. Joseph said to his brothers, "I am Joseph! Is my father still alive?" But his brothers could not answer him, so dismayed were they at his presence.---Genesis 45:1-3

"ANEE YOSEF!!!!"

That's probably what Joseph actually said, as it's the Hebrew for "I am Joseph!" And he probably said it several times.

With these words stark terror comes over the brothers! The one they had wronged two decades ago, the brother they had hurt so much, the brother they had abandoned completely, now stands before them in power. He can kill them all! And there's not one thing they could do about it! Or, at the very least, he could chain them and make them his slaves forever in Egypt. They were completely, utterly, at his mercy.

And they were terrified.

But Joseph is not interested in vengeance.

Then Joseph said to his brothers, "Come closer to me." And they came closer.

He said, "I am your brother, Joseph, whom you sold into Egypt. And now, do not be distressed, or angry with yourselves, because you sold me here; for God sent me before you to preserve life. For the famine has been in the land these two years; and there are five more years in which there will be neither plowing nor harvest. God sent me before you to preserve for you a remnant on earth, and to keep alive for you many survivors. (The New English Bible translates this sentence as "God sent me ahead of you to ensure that you will have descendants on earth, and to preserve you all, a great band of survivors.")

"So it was not you who sent me here, but God; he has made me a father to Pharaoh, and lord of all his house and ruler over all the land of Egypt. Hurry and go up to my father and say to him, 'Thus says your son Joseph: God has made me lord of all Egypt. Come down to me and do not delay. You shall settle in the land of Goshen, and you shall be near me, you and your children and your children's children, as well as your flocks, your herds, and all that you have.

"I will provide for you there--since there are five more years of famine to come--so that you and your household, and all that you have, will not come to poverty.'"

Then he gazed at his brothers and said, "Now your eyes and the eyes of my brother Benjamin see that it is my own mouth that speaks to you. You must tell my father how greatly I am honored in Egypt, and all that you have seen. Hurry!!! Bring my father down here!"

Then he fell upon his brother Benjamin's neck and wept, while Benjamin wept upon his neck. And he kissed all his brothers and wept upon them; and after that his brothers talked with him.   ---Genesis 45:4-15

Joseph completely forgave his brothers. He had become so centered and balanced and so connected to God that his whole attitude had changed. His focus was no longer on what had happened to him, on the pain he had experienced, the hurt, the suffering. He was now focused on the present to prepare for the future. He did not ignore what had happened to him but, by his reliance on God's presence with him, he could now perceive God using even his suffering and pain to bring something good out of what could have been a terrible tragedy.

There's a great deal to think about in this story, for it is offers us one of the most powerful scenes in the Bible when it comes to surprise and reconciliation. I'm sure there are many things this story prompts you to think about, and if that is happening to you as you read this, good for you! Think about these things!!! Ponder them, reflect on them.

Do not discard what you're thinking about, just hold it in one part of your consciousness and let me gently suggest a couple of things that I believe this story prompts us to consider.

First, remember something I've touched on a couple of times. When we move through dark times and then begin our transition into times of lesser darkness, even coming into the light, we have the terrible freedom to choose to march right back into darkness. God is not going to stop us. We can focus on the negative, the dark, the hurt, the suffering we've gone through. We can reflect on these things, ponder them, chew on them over and over, not just for days or months, but for years.

Let me see if I can get at this by sharing with you

my favorite example of what I'm talking about. Did you have to read, in high school or college, Charles Dickens' late work *Great Expectations*? It was one of the great works of literature that was required reading in the high school I attended. I'm so glad this was forced on me because I discovered that I actually enjoyed reading Dickens, even though he could get quite wordy at times. This story of the boy Pip, who has a chance meeting with an escaped convict early in the story, who then grows up to become a gentleman, a man of means and some wealth, even though he was raised in poverty, is a magnificent story of a young man growing up, becoming quite the arrogant snob and then experiencing a transforming experience of self-awareness that moves him into real maturity.

A major part of his decades-long journey into self-awareness and maturity is spent with Miss Havisham and her daughter, Estella. Miss Havisham has always fascinated me for some reason, probably because she is so bizarre! She was jilted by her fiancé, literally left at the altar wearing her bridal dress. This traumatic experience went very, very deep in her, twisting her, turning her away from the bright, cheery young woman ready to be married into a bitter, angry woman who became more so over the years.

Did I mention she was bizarre? How many people do you know who wear their wedding dress all the time as a way of NEVER forgetting her hurt. For years and years and years (plus never changing much of her house from the way it was on the day she was to get married, even to the point of keeping the dry, rotted and molded wedding cake! Ewwwww. . . . She nurtured her pain. Her wedding dress, wearing it every day as it slowly rotted, her house, frozen in time, are powerful symbols of her twisted inner self, her negative attitude to life, and especially her hatred of men.

But Miss Havisham isn't content to keep her bitterness to herself, oh no. She adopts a daughter, and she can because she is quite wealthy, and simply orders her solicitor to secure her a daughter, which, in mid-nineteenth century England, he can and does. Although she says she originally wanted simply to save the girl (named Estella) from experiencing the pain she had, it isn't long until Miss Havisham is coaching and training Estella how to entice young men with her beauty and riches. Estella becomes very, very good at doing what Miss Havisham desires. Like a person fishing allowing the fish to nibble at the bait then sharply pulling the line taut to place the hook into the fish's mouth, so would Estella lead these males on until she knew she had a man absolutely infatuated with her. Then, one day, seemingly out of the blue, for no apparent reason at all, with a beautiful, ever-widening, incredibly cruel smile under eyes that had no expression of remorse whatsoever, break their relationship, shatter it completely, deliberately hurting the guy as much as she could; then slowly, oh so slowly, looking down at him the whole time, turn her back on her would-be husband, seemingly relishing the incredible pain she has just inflicted, enjoying leaving the guy twisting internally much like a fish twists on the line as it is pulled out of the water, and dies. Thus does Miss Havisham extract her vengeance on the male animal that betrayed her.

Of course, Dickens' novel is complex in plot but above all, it is an amazingly in-depth exploration of the inner and outer character and relationships among the main persons in the novel, primarily Pip, Estella, and Miss Havisham. Plus, as in all of Charles Dickens' works, the story involves dozens of different, colorful and occasionally grotesque characters. Which is what makes reading Dickens so much fun! But I hope you perceive my point. Miss Havisham never (at least until the last part of the story) lets go of her hurt. And by nurturing this hurt, feeding it every day, always, always, always thinking about it, feeling it again, and again, she corrupts her beloved, adopted daughter.

This seems to be the way things are, in that when we keep our hurt, never letting it go, we make a profound different on those closest to us in negative ways. I doubt any of us would go as far as Miss Havisham, but we will have some sort of effect on them, most often our family.

Crazy as it seems, God loves us enough to give us the freedom to be miserable if we want to. It's all up to us. It really is in this case. Are we willing to let go hurt feelings enough to let the Spirit begin leading us into something new, or do we clutch them close, really holding tightly on to them?

Do we want to live? Do we really want to get on with our life? We may say we do, but we keep going back to the hurtful events over and over and over in our minds. It's like we're in a boat trying its best to move away from a dock that's on fire. But the very short line that ties us to the dock is still tied. We can cut it quickly, we can even untie it slowly and then move out into safer water. But the point is, if we keep a line tied to the dock that's burning, then the fire that destroys the dock will eventually begin to consume us in our boat. The fire of hate, of resentment, of disappointment, if we keep ourselves tied to it, will eventually consume us.

Secondly, we need to remember that forgiving someone who has hurt us deeply is not easy. Also, if we have hurt someone deeply, and we know we have hurt this person, who is our friend, our loved one, a member of our family, it is unfair for us to expect that other to forgive us quickly.

The truth all of us know, we know this so, so well, is that forgiveness takes time.

Real forgiveness is always a two-step process, namely if we are the culprit and we ask the one we've hurt to forgive us, we have to take the second step before we can expect any sort of forgiveness to be expressed. Second step? What second step?

Ah.

You see, that's the problem, and I think it comes from what we experienced growing up as kids, and, in turn, how we have taught our children to forgive. Do you remember how it was when we got caught doing something wrong, or hurting our sibling our of anger or spite or because we just wanted to? Dad or mom of the baby-sitter or the nanny or grandmother or grandfather would make us confront the one we wronged, and we'd hear those awful words, "Now. . . APOLOGIZE!"

Yes, apologize. . . say the magic words, "I'm sorry."

Not because we are but because we got caught!

If we hadn't been caught, there's no way we would have apologized. We knew it was wrong, what we did; but we didn't care. We were so angry! So frustrated! So hurt! The feelings were just boiling over inside us. So, we said cruel things, we hit, we slammed things around and broke something, or maybe we broke something intentionally because we knew it was her, it was his, favorite, and it make a terrific SMASH when it broke, a sound that delighted us.

Sorry? I should say not!

But, because Dad or Mom or whoever is standing over us, and they're a whole lot bigger so we say the words.

And things go on. Our parents moves back into their universe of adults and we move on into our childhood stuff. By now we may actually begin to feel a bit of remorse about clobbering our little brother or sister or deliberately breaking their favorite toy because we really don't like it when he/she starts to cry and, truth be told, we didn't really want to hurt him. . . well, maybe not too much. . . But at any rate, we're still not sorry we did what we did. . . not yet anyway. . .

Do you get it? Because this is the way we were taught to forgive someone, we tend to have this experience operating somewhere inside of us, and when hurt someone, intentionally or otherwise, and we regret it, we often go to the person and say, "Please forgive me. I'm sorry."

We expect the other to say, "OK, but don't do that again, that hurt," just like it used to be when we were kids. But then the other person does not immediately say the magic words, and it surprises us. What's going on? We've apologized! What more does she/he want, for cryin' out loud! Groveling? Not going to happen!!!

The truth is it is grossly unfair to expect someone to express forgiveness when all we've done is ask for it.

Okay, you say, I suppose that makes sense. But what more can we do?

That's the second step I mentioned. Real forgiveness never will occur unless this second step is put into place.

This second step goes like this. When we have hurt someone we have to accept the pain of acknowledging we have hurt this person deeply, and because we have inflicted such deep hurt, we cannot be as close as we used to be and we most certainly cannot expect the other person to behave as if nothing has happened. We have to be willing to accept the consequences of our actions. This means we have to be willing to experience distance, perhaps even coldness, from that person we have wronged. We have to be willing to be alienated in some fashion from that person. Hopefully, not forever. Hopefully only for a while. But we never know. That's the really hard thing. The pain that goes deep, deep into us is facing the horrible truth that we may have damaged this relationship beyond any hope of reconciliation. And there's nothing we can do about this. No matter how many words we say in apologizing, no matter how many times we say it, no matter what we buy or do to show our remorse (although they may help a bit, it's true), we cannot change another person's mind.

And this is hard, oh, is it ever hard. After we have done what we've done, and seen the pain this has brought to the other, why, just like when we saw our smaller siblings start to cry from what we did to them, we begin to experience remorse; we begin to regret what we've done. We begin to experience pain. And we don't like it, nosiree, not at all.

So, we're going to do something about it, we're going to apologize and set things right. So we do, and do, and do, and keep on doing. Only the truth is, things cannot be set right again. . . at least, not for a while.

Christians have an extremely difficult time with this, not just because of the way we were taught to forgive, but because of what our Lord said to Peter and twelve about forgiving. Peter asks Jesus, "Lord, how often must I forgive my brother when he asks? Seven times?" (Which is what the rabbinic law advocated) Jesus's famous reply? Seventy times seven. (Matthew 18:21-22) In other words, if your offended brother/friend/etc. asks for forgiveness, always grant it.

Because Jesus is coming at this not from the viewpoint of the one doing the hurting but from the one hurt, and he knows oh-so-well how carrying a grudge, holding on to hurts, can damage our souls. This is what Jesus is getting at.

But we tend to read this as the key to Christian behavior, and therefore we Christians forgive one another because we have been forgiven. And so, when we mess up and hurt someone close, and we ask for forgiveness, we expect to be forgiven, and quickly, because that is what Jesus said to do. And when such forgiveness is slow in coming, we start to accuse the other of holding a grudge, of never being able to turn off her memory, of him never forgetting anything. . . WE'VE tried, Lord knows, but this other person. . . . sheesh. . .

Such an attitude reveals just how little this offender has recognized the real hurt inflicted, and in not recognizing this, then disrespecting the other person as a living, feeling human being whom they have terribly hurt. What we Christians overlook so many times when we're dealing with forgiving someone or asking for forgiveness is the hurt involved, and the corresponding necessity of the offender being willing first, to acknowledge his/her wrongdoing, and then being willing to bear the consequences of such wrongdoing, namely the distancing resulting from the offense, the pulling away, the coldness, the alienation.

We Christians tend to collapse this whole, in-depth, involved process among human beings that is complex and intricate, into a simple statement and expected response. Apologize. Then forgive. And everything's just hunky-dory again.

NO!!!! IT'S NOT. People have been hurt, for cryin' out loud. . . there's been a lot of pain. . . It's just like when we're clumsy and hit our shins, or our knees, or our arms on something and it hurts like crazy. Then, in just a few minutes, we see a bruise start to appear. It takes a good while for this bruise to go away. So it is with the pain we feel when someone hurts us. It's just like a bruise, it takes a while for this pain to move away from the center of our thinking.

And that's what we shy away from, pain. We seriously do not want to accept pain. And especially do we not want to accept the pain of long, deep friendship, even love, dying. We just do not want to believe that we have killed what was so precious, what was so important. . . a relationship that was so close. . . a love that lasted for years, decades even. . . a respect that had been so hard-won...

My point?   Forgiveness is a process that takes a while. And, depending on the hurt involved, perhaps a very long time. And, because I want to be honest here, the forgiveness longed for may never, ever come, because the hurt is just too deep.

You see, for real forgiveness to occur, there has to be an acknowledgement of real wrongdoing; that's step one. Then there has to be a serious recognition of the deep pain involved and, along with this recognition a willingness to accept the real, serious consequences that flow from all this. This is the second step.

If you do not understand this, you do not understand forgiveness.

I'm sitting in a pew in the sanctuary close to the front. I'm about to be installed as the new Designated (or long-term interim) pastor for this church. I'm listening to my colleagues as they lead the congregation in the Presbyterian service of installation for the newly called pastor. In our tradition both clergy and lay people are to take part in leading such a service. One of my colleagues has given a great sermon on the work of the minister in a way that was creative and challenging for me and the congregation I had been called to serve. Following the sermon, I had been called to the front and other colleagues and lay people had read to me and the congregation the installation questions from the Book of Order, our by-laws, so to speak. Another colleague had given me the official "charge", that is, words of encouragement and reminding me of my ordination vow in ways appropriate to my new work in this congregation, with all the challenges they and

I were facing together.

Then I sat back in my pew and looked to the lectern where another of my colleagues began to give the "charge" to the congregation. She had been an active, ordained minister for several decades now, and, for close to twenty years, had been active as an interim pastor in this particular presbytery (what we call a specific geographic area containing a number of Presbyterian churches; truthfully, it's another name for 'diocese') She had also been an interim to the congregation I was starting to serve; not immediately prior to my coming, but some years before, a 'couple of preachers' ago, as we tend to say.

Because she knew these people, she got more personal than what I have usually heard from those giving such 'charges'. She named, in a general way, some of the problems that had been going on in the church, and then she went on to say a few sentences about how mean, nasty and hurtful people had been to one another in this congregation.

I winced a bit, but knew it to be true, and was more than a tad grateful for her willingness to name some of the elephants in this particular room. But then she said something that astounded me, and changed forever how I interpreted a particular passage of scripture, and even shifted something of my Christology, i.e. the doctrine of Jesus Christ as incarnate Son of God. She said she realized Christians are to forgive one another, even when it's hard, but when it actually turns out to be HARD, then we tend to quit trying. And quit coming to church. Or even leave. "Please remember," she said (and here it comes), "that Jesus said as he was being nailed to the cross, 'Father, forgive them, for they know not what they do.' But don't get the idea that Jesus was forgiving those who were crucifying him right then and there. No. He was saying, Father! YOU forgive them, because right now, I can't. I'm hurting too much."

I know Sally went on to say something like keep on trying to forgive, and when you cannot, then give it to God, like Jesus; I know she said something like this because she told me she did when we got together for coffee sometime later and I brought up what she had said. But sitting there, in that sanctuary that Sunday evening, years ago, I heard very little of what came after. My mind was whirling too much to pay attention to what came after.

Father, you forgive them. . . . Because right now, I cannot. . . .

An idiosyncratic interpretation, I'll grant you, and perhaps theologically out of whack with Luke, for after all, when Stephen is stoned in Acts, he prays the same prayer as Jesus, praying that God will not hold this sin (i.e. stoning him to death) against them.

That's fine. But what my very astute colleague did for me personally was make me aware as I had never been before that if Jesus was truly human, then his experience of the betrayal and abandonment of the disciples, the hate of the soldiers, the hate of the crowd, the cold indifference from the religious leaders who most understood him and rejected him, his whole hope for the kingdom now smashed. . . .to say that "I know I should forgive, but right now, Father, I cannot at this very second, because I'm hurting too much." That Jesus said he, at that moment of his tortured, hurting life, could not forgive, whew. . . It may not be strictly theologically correct, and the thinking part of me is jumping on the conclusion that if Jesus could not forgive at that moment, then perhaps there are other moments he cannot forgive, and if he cannot forgive, then perhaps he is not divine after all, but more a mortal man than we realized. . . (and, I ask myself, does the ancient heresy of Apollinarianism, that Jesus did not have a completely human consciousness but only a divine consciousness, raise it's head here?) Such statements, such assertions definitely make us think.

We can talk about whether or not Jesus might have meant this in his words, Father forgive them. What I am in no doubt about it is that to offer such an interpretation is definitely true to the spirit of the three synoptic gospels, Matthew, Mark and Luke, in their portrayal of Jesus's agony in the garden, when he said, "let this cup pass from me. . . but not as I will, but as you, Father, will. . .", their portrayal of Jesus as a human being. Orthodox Christians affirm that Jesus was truly human, in body and in mind, that is, in consciousness. Every part, every aspect of him, was human. And every part, every aspect of him, was also divine.

This is a great mystery, and one that I acknowledge in faith.

Because I do acknowledge the true humanity of Jesus, I also know that the truth of forgiveness is something God takes with amazing seriousness. He knows the pain, and what my friend's interpretation called me to recognize, is that God himself knows how incredibly hard it is to forgive when we are deeply hurt. God himself take this pain seriously because Jesus felt this pain, all the way down. And then took this pain into the Godhead itself when he ascended into heaven. What a man felt, what a human being feels, both great joy and great pain, is now part of God himself, because Jesus of Nazareth, a human being who lived, who was happy, who was sad, who was joyful and who experienced terrible betrayal and pain, this man is now part of God himself.

One last thing.

People of faith have always said that God's purpose for our lives is a gracious purpose, that God wants us to experience joy, wants us to be fulfilled. After all, Jesus said, "I have come that you might have life, and have it more abundantly." (John 10: 10)

That being the case, then why is there so much pain? Why do we have so much hurt in our lives, so much tragedy?

Because God loves us and the world so much that he gives us seriously scary freedom. It's when we, and others, abuse this freedom, that the pain comes, most often. Of course there are also the tragedies of the world that crash upon us. Car wrecks, shootings, abuse, rapes, murders. Where is God when these things happen? That's our question, right? And we like to affirm, God is right there, right with us when these terrible things happen, right?

Somehow, though, I have a feeling that when Joseph was being sold into slavery, as he looked at his brothers from the cage, or being tied up by the caravan drivers, looked at his brothers calmly turning their backs on him for what he firmly believed was forever, I somehow doubt that Joseph thought God was with him.

The presence of God is probably the opposite of

what he thought: God is not here. God is nowhere to be found. If God was here, he would have stopped my brothers from selling me. But that didn't happen. No one stopped them betraying me. No one stopped them from lying to my father Jacob about me.

God, here? Don't make me laugh. . .

That's exactly what it feels like. . . when we've been betrayed. . . terrible, horrible things happen to us and to our loved ones. . . . God is nowhere around. . . . if He was, he would have done something to stop this terrible tragedy. Don't tell me God was there, because even if he was, it doesn't matter because HE DID NOTHING!!!!!

But that's not true, is it. . .

God is there. . . in the tragedy. . . .in the pain. . . .

God is with us. . . all the way. . . in all the hurt. . . .

Joseph said to his brother some of the most remarkable words in all of scripture: You meant this for evil, but God turned it to good.

The brothers sold Joseph into slavery out of spite, out of 'evil'. But God then utilized Joseph's character, his innate sense of right and wrong, his willingness to be responsible and to hope. . . God used this to bring Joseph into contact with Pharaoh at precisely the right time to save hundreds, thousands of people, including Joseph's own family, and to reunite this family.

I do think that we perceive the providence of God, God's care, God working in our lives, most aptly in timing. That is to say, in how things either come together, or how we are brought by circumstances into contact with people and opportunities that end up making profound differences for good in our and in others' lives. We come together, we encounter events and openings, opportunities at a particular point in our life, and it makes all the difference in the world. This is how God cares for us and how he most often works directly in our lives.

How does God do this?

Don't know.

We're not dealing with puppets here. We're dealing with human beings, who have freedom, who can do what they want when they want. And yet, somehow, someway, Joseph is brought into contact with Pharaoh, who dreamed his dreams . . .

Remember, please, Joseph had been waiting for over two years. . .

God's timing, though, is absolutely impeccable.

If we trust him.

This is how God works. . . somehow, someway, things happen. . .

Joseph's life, his whole life, points to this, and finally, FINALLY! We have proof positive that this mysterious way of working in people's lives IS the way God works. What proof?

The cross.

The ultimate tragedy. The ultimate betrayal. The ultimate abandonment.

God takes this great, this immense evil, and turns it into the greatest blessing and truth ever known: death is swallowed up in victory, the victory of the resurrection. This IS how God works. This IS how God turns evil to good. This IS how things are for

God's people, so hope... HOPE in the midst of death...
HOPE in the midst of tragedy..

This is where Paul is coming from when he writes over in Romans 8: 28: "We know that in everything God works for good with those who love him, who are called according to his purpose."

So many times we can read this and immediately think, "Yeah, tell that to the Holocaust victims." Or, "Yeah, tell that to those children we prayed for in church last week who lost their mom and dad in a car accident when a drunk driver crossed into their lane and hit them head on."

We say, "God is not there. It was an accident, and horrible, and I'm so glad things like that won't happen in heaven."

Or, more darkly, "God is not there, and I know he's not there because there is no God. If God was there, then he'd have done something . . . and Jesus was a first century prophet, and maybe he rose from the dead and ascended into heaven, but that has absolutely nothing to do with me. And, above all, that was a long, long time ago. . . and I haven't seen any more dead men walking around."

We have the terrible freedom to believe these words to be true. OR, we can ponder how God worked in Joseph's life, which we now can see is a paradigm, a template, for how God works in people's lives. . . unseen. . . unfelt a lot of times. . . especially when we go through darkness and more darkness.

But then, because we trust, because we still live as God's people, trusting him, trusting Jesus, we discover that God's timing touches us, and things change. . . for the better!!!! We change too!!!!!

This isn't a fairy tale, or a bit of profound, hard-won wisdom. It is the truth. The real truth. And we know this because of Jesus. All he said, all he did, and above all, his taking the pain of the cross onto himself and then rising from the dead, thus vindicating all of his deeds and words, this Jesus is alive and in us through his Spirit in us. (II Corinthians 1: 4-5 and 21-22)

This is the whole key: by the Spirit with us, alive and working in us, we have the power to HOPE in times of darkness. . . . because we know the darkness shall be overcome. . . . because Jesus rose from the darkness of death and hell itself. Because he did this, we dare to hope now, we dare to trust him now, we dare to rely on him now, in the midst of so much that hurts, that rips and tears at us, that smashes us down again and again.

Alcohol, drugs, betrayal, accidents, tragedies of horrible kinds. . . .

WE CAN TAKE IT, WE CAN ENDURE, WE CAN EXPERIENCE LIGHT AGAIN. AND SOMEHOW, IN SOME MYSTERIOUS WAY KNOWN ONLY TO GOD, GOD, IN HIS INCREDIBLE TIMING, ACTS UPON US, CHANGES US, TRANSFORMS US, TRANSFORMS OUR LIVES, CHANGES THINGS TOTALLY AROUND INTO SOMETHING THAT BRINGS A BLESSING INSTEAD OF A CURSE...

Because of Jesus.

All. . . all because of Jesus Christ.

This is why Paul says, "For I am certain that neither DEATH nor LIFE. . .

Not angels, nor principalities, (whatever they are)

> Nothing that happens to us in life,
>
> Nothing that can happen to us in the future,
>
> No power in life,
>
> No matter how great or how small,
>
> No matter how overwhelming,
>
> Nothing in this universe, NOTHING
>
> Will ever separate us from the love and power (not just feeling or being empathetic, but actually doing things for us) of God revealed in Christ Jesus our Lord!
>
> ----Romans 8:38-39

The Story of Joseph
How God Works in Our Lives

CHAPTER NINE

Reconnecting

We've come to the conclusion of this story about Joseph, a great story that deals with God's mysterious way of working in our lives. Truth be told, for Christians, this story actually foreshadows the mystery of the cross

Yes, there are some more verses in dealing with Joseph and Jacob in Genesis, but these are relatively minor episodes, even though the death of Jacob is within these additional episodes. Nevertheless, the real end of this story arc is when this family reconnects, when it is reunited.

When the report was heard in Pharaoh's house, "Joseph's brothers have come," Pharaoh and his servants were pleased. Pharaoh said to Joseph, "Say to your brothers, "Do this: load your animals and go back to the land of Canaan. Take your father and your households and come to me, so that I may give you the best of the land of Egypt, and you may enjoy the fat of the land." You are further charged to say, "Do this: take wagons from the land of Egypt for your little ones and for your wives, and bring your father and come. Give no thought to your possessions, for the best of all the land of Egypt

is yours."---Genesis 45:16-20

How generous of Pharaoh! This says a lot about this particular king of Egypt, who was wise and caring to his people, and to those who worked for him. Pharaoh's response also reveals that he and Joseph have a close relationship that continued through the rest of their lives.

The sons of Israel did so. Joseph gave them wagons according to the instruction of Pharaoh, and he gave them provisions for the journey. To each one of them he gave a set of garments; but to Benjamin he gave three hundred pieces of silver and five sets of garments! To his father he sent the following: ten donkeys loaded with the good things of Egypt, and ten female donkeys loaded with grain, bread and provision for his father on the journey. Then he sent his brothers on their way, and as they were leaving he said to them, "Do not quarrel along the way."--- Genesis 45:21-24

Joseph's brothers may have grown up, but they were still brothers. Do not quarrel along the way!!! He knows them well.

When you're young, you and your siblings often seem to be fighting all the time; at least that's true for a lot of us. But then we grow up and, hopefully, we get along better.

Yet there are still times when, because of stress, or the fact that we're all back together after a long time of being apart, we slip back into the rolls we had when we were much younger.

I've often noticed that when families get back together at holidays, for instance Thanksgiving or Christmas, they will fall back into the rolls they had growing up. The oldest, who is an Executive Vice-President for a company, becomes his bossy self again, blatantly telling his brothers and sisters what they should do about things, something he would never, ever do with his colleagues at a board meeting. The youngest, who is now a noted brain surgeon, starts to defuse things by making jokes, and being sarcastic, something he does somewhat with his colleagues, but never to the extent he now engages in. And the investment banker, the second born, who has made a lot of money because he was willing to take chances when others weren't starts to play the rebel, and, just like when they were teenagers, begins to deliberately antagonize his older brother. Who, in turn, rises to this baiting like a brook trout to a fishing lure.

It's fascinating to me how our roles in the family still proscribe so much of our adult behavior and how easily we fall into these roles unconsciously, especially when we're with our brothers and sisters as a group.

Joseph seems to be aware of this dynamic in challenging his brothers not to argue with one another. After all, he is the one who was wronged, and he has forgiven them. What have they to quarrel about anyway?

But we're human beings and when we're under stress we tend to become contentious. And times of transitions, even good transitions, are times of tension. We need to be sure the bills are properly paid, the necessary documents signed and that our income is adequate during our transition and beyond. But sometimes we can focus on the change so much that any good coming from the transition fades.

Plus, for so many of us, when we get worried or fearful or scared, we get angry. We lash out with words at those closest to us and then we feel guilty. After a while the transition becomes not a new opportunity, but a massive headache.

The Hebrew word for quarrel that Joseph uses is an excellent word to remember during transitions. Let me translate it literally: "Do not be perturbed," or, more to the point, "Do not let yourself become agitated." That is to say, do not allow yourself to give in to your tensions, to your anxieties.

You know what you're like, implies Joseph to his brothers. So, be aware of that. Focus on the good. Be practical. Be realistic. Don't allow yourself to slip into behavior that will prompt tension, anxiety and harsh words. Always keep in focus the good, the real opportunity available through the transition you're going through.

So they went up out of Egypt and came to their father Jacob in the land of Canaan. And they told him, "Joseph is still alive! He is even ruler over all the land of Egypt."

Jacob was stunned. He could not believe his sons.

But, when they told him all the words of Joseph that he had said to them, and when he saw the wagons that Joseph had sent to carry him, the spirit of their father, Jacob, revived. He said to them, "Enough! My son Joseph is still alive. I must go and see him before I

die.”---Genesis 45: 25-28

The old man nearly fainted when the boys returned and told him all that had happened. Had trouble believing them at first, but then he looked outside and saw all the donkeys loaded down with what Joseph had sent.

His son was alive! Joseph was alive!!!!!

“I am going to see my son again before I die!”

When Jacob set out on his journey with all that he had and came to beer-Sheba, he offered sacrifices to the God of his father Isaac. God spoke to him in visions of the night and said, “Jacob! Jacob!”

And Jacob said, “Here I am.”

Then God said, “I am God, the God of your father; do not be afraid to go down to Egypt, for I will make of you a great nation there. I myself will go down with you to Egypt, and I will also bring you up again, and Joseph’s own hand shall close your eyes.”---Genesis 46: 1-4

This is very interesting. The first night during the move Jacob has a dream/vision. In this vision/dream the Lord tells him that it is all right to go to Egypt.

Of course it’s all right to go to Egypt! His son is the man in charge there! Why wouldn’t it be all right? Why would this be in the text?

The obvious reason is that Jacob was probably more anxious about making this journey than he let on. After all, he was quite old at this point, and he didn’t travel as well as he used to. In fact, the trip, which would have lasted at least a week or more, was dangerous to somebody who was as old as Jacob was. Traveling in a bumpy wagon with no springs is hard on such a man. He could take one, maybe even two days but a whole week? Or more? It's a real possibility that he could have a heart attack or a stroke. So, even though the text does not say this specifically, I think it's safe to assume that Jacob had been praying about this, asking the Lord to help him survive this journey.

Also, please note that this isn't a visit; it's a relocation of everybody. Jacob is not just visiting Joseph, he's moving to Egypt to be with Joseph. He's leaving all the security and comfort of a place/area he's lived in his whole life.

Yes, Joseph said he would take care of him, take care of all of them, all of his brothers, their wives, their children, etc. etc. That's all well and good. But they would all be living in a different place, surrounded by different people; they would now be foreigners living in a foreign place.

If you have had to contemplate such a move you can appreciate Jacob's anxiety. The joyful moments of hearing that Joseph was alive and inviting all of them to come live with him were earlier in the day or the day(s) previous. Now, though, in the night, when Jacob is alone with his thoughts and things have calmed down, and everybody is in his or her own tent/room or whatever, anxious thoughts start to creep in.

It won't be the same. . . will be very different. . . how will we deal with the Egyptians, and they with us. . . will we be happy. . . . will things go all right. . .

Thinking such thoughts are normal, and most of us who have moved have had similar ones. It's understandable that Jacob would be anxious about such a move, and pray about this to the Lord.   These are the obvious reasons that this incident is included in the story.

But there is a less obvious, more subtle, and actually more important reason. This reason goes back to the promise God made with Jacob, and with Jacob's father Isaac, and Isaac's father Abraham. It's about the promise of God to the patriarchs to make their offspring a great nation, and to give to their offspring the land to which Abraham came when he left Ur all those many years ago.

If Jacob moves to Egypt, what becomes of this great promise? Does this move negate this promise? Is Jacob interfering with, perhaps even blocking, God's will by moving to Egypt? Should he stay right where he is so that God could fulfill what he promised to him? After all, he has a lot of sons; Joseph is only one. And God's promise is to all of his sons. So Jacob has a divine obligation to his other sons to make sure God's promise to them remains in force. What is he to do?

God tells Jacob, in this night vision/dream, to proceed with his plans to move to Egypt and that His promise will remain in force. In fact, the promise to make of Jacob's offspring a great nation will actually come to pass while they are in Egypt. Then there is a most amazing statement: the Lord says I myself will go with you to Egypt.

To us who are Christians and thus perceive the presence of God through the Holy Spirit that was given to all disciples and followers of Jesus after Jesus rose from the dead, such an assertion is a truism: God goes with us wherever we go, and goes with us in and through the Spirit.

But, in Jacob's time, and for most of the Old Testament, the presence of God is tied directly to the land on which God's people are living. Move the people away from the land on which God revealed himself to them and called them to worship him, and you move away from the presence of God. (See II Kings 5:15-19, with Naaman, responding to Elisha's curing him of leprosy, wanting to take back soil from Palestine so that he could worship the God of Israel in his own country. See also the great psalm of lament concerning the people's exile after Babylon conquered Jerusalem, Psalm 137)

For God to say specifically that he was going to be with his servant Jacob, and Jacob's offspring in a foreign land was an amazing promise. But God does not stop there. He also promises Jacob that He will bring Jacob's offspring out of Egypt and back to place Jacob is leaving. Which we, knowing the whole Old Testament story of Israel, know that God is foretelling what will happen with Moses and the Exodus, which is several hundred years later.

For most biblical scholars these verses have been inserted into this story, a story told and retold over centuries, from long after the Exodus events. It's a prophesy, but a prophesy only in a literary way because the writer knows what's going to happen in the future (the Exodus and the conquest of the promised land) because the narrator is writing this down in a time nearly a thousand years after the Exodus. This may or may not be true (so many biblical scholars seem to have a built-in disposition to doubt anything supernatural, always looking for a rational explanation for a seemingly supernatural happening); there's no way we can sit down with the author of Genesis and ask about this. Rather than to debate whether or not this is actual prophesy, a far better approach is to ask the simple question, what's this little section doing here, in this part of the narrative? How might it be important to the overall story?

We've already begun to answer this. In these verses God is saying to Jacob, Don't worry. I will be with you.

I have you. I will take care of you and yours, and I will never forget my promise to you. Cease your worries. Go see your son. Let him look after you now in your old age. That's the first thing these verses mean, and the second emerges from God's promise to be with Jacob. The unknown stretches before Jacob. Jacob cannot see how the promises of God will work out. To his old eyes it even seems like the end of the promise. He's leaving the very land that God promised to him and his children. How will these children come to have this land again? Jacob cannot perceive how this will come to pass, but the Lord promises that it will. And Jocob does trust the Lord, and the Lord gently told him to not be afraid. The promise about the land to the children of Jacob will be fulfilled. The promise is still in force. Things will work out all right.

Does this have anything to do us today?

I think so. What I take away from this is that in those times when we are faced with major decisions, decisions that may have been forced on us by circumstances, like accepting a new job that fits our skills and talents, a job that comes our way after we have been forced from a previous one, but entails a difficult relocation, always we are called to remember that God in Jesus Christ goes with us wherever we go. We may very well be called by the Spirit into such a new opportunity.

Trust the goodness of God and live for him, making our decisions out of a deep confidence in God's goodness to us and leading us into new opportunities. When opportunities come our way, opportunities for employment when we are unemployed, opportunities for advancement, opportunities that will help us move forward, opportunities that will help our families, then, like Jacob, we are called to trust the Lord. Trust that the Lord will be with us wherever we go, whatever we do, as long as we live for him. He will be with us, and will bless us and bring good out of the most difficult and trying circumstances.

I've mentioned relocating, to new jobs, to new opportunities stemming from new employment sometimes in the same city we're living in, sometimes requiring moving to a different city. This parallels the text because what will happen to us in making such a new beginning is unknown and filled with ambiguities. But such ambiguous futures are not limited to new jobs and having to relocate because of the job. The truth is we share Jacob's anxieties anytime we are faced with moving into new areas of our lives, areas that are different, unknown. It could be we are dealing with our anxiety about entering into a new relationship after a breakup with the one we honestly thought God had chosen for us, perhaps even after we had been married for a long time to the one we thought we'd be married to until we died.

Sometimes we are led to a radical new beginning. And this can be a very anxious thing, maybe even frightening. What I mean by a *radical* new beginning is that this new opportunity, this new situation, perhaps even this new person, is really, really different than what has gone before for us; yet, there are so many similarities also. It is the different aspects of what we will have to undergo that makes us pause and wonder: am I doing the right thing? Is this REALLY what God wants me to do?

I faced this when I was wrestling with whether or not to take a position at a congregation all the way across the country. I had grown up in North Carolina, gone to high school and college there, then graduate school in Virginia. With the sole exception of serving a few years in western Kentucky, my entire career as a minister was in North Carolina and Virginia. But now, now I was single after a long marriage. I could go where I felt called to go. But my daughters, all four of them, were now adult women, one married, three in school, and they were all in Virginia. No, I didn't see them every day, but I did several times a month, and, of course, on every major holiday. There had never been a time when I had not. Also, the family I had left, on both my father and mother's side, the few cousins I had kept up with over the years, they were all in North and South Carolina. And finally, all, ALL of the friends I had in the world were in these two states. I had no family out west. I had no friends out west. I knew no one out west. I would not be able to see my daughters, my family, my friends when I wanted to, when I needed to. I would not be able to get in my car and meet them somewhere for coffee, to chat, or go over to their place or have them to mine, just to see them and enjoy their company and wisdom. Sure, there were phones, and computers (remember, this was before the pandemic through which we all became experienced at connecting with others via our computers and tablets), but this was just not the same as being in each other's company. More on the edgy side, for I knew this was a seriously complicated situation I was being asked to deal with, colleagues whom I respected and with whom I saw regularly for discussions about how to deal with various church complications, and to whom I looked for encouragement and support, they would be nowhere near me. The more I thought about this call, this move, the more things I began to think of that would be taken away from me. I actually began to feel a bit scared.

And then, out of the blue, I received a call from the presbytery exec (the presbyterian version of a bishop, sort of) requesting me to consider going to a large congregation not too far away that could use my skills and experience, as they were having some major conflict.

My, my my! I thought. Here's the answer I was looking for. A church to serve that was here, in the area where I lived. No need to move all at once, it could be done via several trips. No need to drive across the country. No need to worry about being able to get together with family, with friends, with colleagues. The answer to all my concerns, right?

At first, I certainly thought so. But something was brushing lightly over my senses, that something was. . . well, not right is too clear. More like hearing oh so faintly a jarring note in a chord. For the life of me, I couldn't put my finger on it. It was too faint. But it gave me pause, enough pause to continue my praying, to continue seeking out friends and a couple of colleagues that I greatly valued their thinking and common sense.

I wrestled and wrestled with all of this, day and night, for well over a week. Then I accepted the offer from the church out west. Yes, it was not going to be an easy move across the country. And driving a 27 ft truck packed to its ceiling, towing my car and coping with my cat, Jazz, was definitely not going to be easy. And not being able to get with my daughters, my friends, my close colleagues, when I wanted and needed to, was going to be hard. But I knew, after my time of wondering, that despite this, it was right to accept this new call to serve this church out west. There was something about the church the presbytery exec wanted me to go to that was not right for me. I had no idea what it was. According to the Exec the church would pay me more money than the church out west. That was awfully tempting. But I could not shake the sense that this particular church was not for me. The exec was really surprised when I called and told him I was moving to the west. "I thought you'd take the higher salary," he said. Normally I would, I replied, in a heartbeat. But not this time. It was only some time later that I discovered that there had been a miscommunication with the exec regarding the salary to be offered. The true salary was substantially less than what I was told. In fact, it was less than what the church out west offered me.

Moving to The West, specifically to Reno, NV, is one of the best things I've ever done. I made new friends, friends that are now friends for life, and with whom I keep up now that I've moved back east. I was able to serve the church in ways that fit me, and, in turn, that church was a real blessing to me. I also discovered new things about myself that has since served me very, very well. The work I and so many others in the church did out there was good work, solid work, lasting work. It quite literally was one of those experiences where it feels as if you'd been preparing for this your whole life. Every learning, every skill, every talent I possessed was needed, and utilized to the best of my ability. It ended up being a truly wonderful, even transformative experience for me. This is not to say that all my time there was great. It wasn't. Are all, every single one of our days glorious? Of course not! There were definitely some evenings in my first year out west that I wondered if I had made the right choice. But I hung in there, and before too long, I knew I had indeed made the right choice.

So, how do we know if it's right for us to move into a radical new beginning?

The best advice I have to offer is what Jacob does when he is faced with this: go to the Lord in prayer, and listen, listen, listen!!! To your instincts, your inner gut, to what the Holy Spirit is saying to you deep, deep within yourself. Listen carefully to your closest friends and relatives. It's important, as I have said previously, to share with those whom we really trust, our hopes and dreams and fears. Listen to them and put what they tell you into dialogue with what you are perceiving from within yourself.

This is what I did. I had done similar praying and listening at various times in my life, but this time I was extremely intentional about everything I did and very, very focused. It took me over a week to begin to discern some things. And when I did, what I began to discern was not something crystal clear and obvious. It's hard to put into words what I perceived. The closest I can come is that it began to feel right that I accept this offer. Along with this faint sense came a slight lessening in my anxiety when I thought about taking the offer and what it would entail. Slight. But enough for me to realize this. When these faint feelings, these faint glimmerings of an answer to what I'd been praying for very intensely for several days, throughout each day, when these faint feelings did not go away every time I brought the question (to move or not) to mind, I slowly began to realize that it was right for me to accept this offer.

I questioned this at first, returning to pray, to talk with God. I went over and over what the few friends I had shared with had said to me. I read the Psalms and paid attention. I paid attention every time I watched TV and to casual conversations, to perceive anything that might help me, that might point a way for me. These things helped. But again, everything was faint, much like a very, very quiet whisper.

It was only after I had concluded that I was called to move that I realized I had experienced something of what had happened to the prophet Elijah when he, in great fear and great frustration, ran and hid in a cave on the Mountain of God (Horeb or Mt. Sinai). He was frightened because the Queen had issued a warrant for his arrest so he could be killed. And no one opposed this. No one seemed to care, at least that's what Elijah thought. So, running for his life, he went to the Mountain of God, wanting to talk to God about what was happening to him and what he should do. He waited for God to answer. At first there was a great fire, then great wind and earthquake. This was how God had first spoken to his people through Moses when Moses ascended the mountain to receive the Ten Commandments. Lots of pyrotechnical effects, lots of noise, lots of ground shaking. That seemed to be the way God communicated to His people. But Elijah had not perceived God to be in the fire, the wind, the earthquake. So he continued to sit in his cave and to wait. And wait. And wait.   Then Elijah heard "a voice of thin stillness". (What in the world does that mean????????) Not something explosively big, not something easily seen twenty miles away. Not something felt so strongly that no one could mistake what was happening. No, none of these. A thin, very, very, very quiet voice. And Elijah listened. And he perceived that God was speaking to him in this very quiet, very faint voice that he could barely make out. And God supported Elijah, God strengthened Elijah and God helped Elijah to make a new beginning. He also let the prophet know that there were more who supported him than he ever realized. He wasn't alone.

Like I said, it was only much later that I realized I had had something of a similar experience in seeking the guidance of the Lord. By responding positively to that faint sense that I was supposed to go and serve that church so far away, a church in such a different area than I had ever experienced and so was perhaps different culturally than what I was used to, a church that would require a lot of effort to get to and to continue to serve, when I said yes to this faint sense, accepting this call and moving west, I ended up being blessed. Really, really blessed.

The Lord will somehow speak to you. Trust me on this. The Lord will guide you. You very well may, and most probably, will have to proceed one step at a time, one day at a time for a good while. After all, it's a new start. A start. A beginning. An opening to something better. Not what will be, not yet. But the first steps to that.

It's called, after all, living in faith, living in trust, living in confidence in Jesus Christ and our Heavenly Father. Right? Right.

So, Jacob goes to Egypt.

Then Jacob set out from Beer-sheba; and the sons of Jacob carried their father, their little ones and their wives in the wagons that Pharaoh had sent to carry them. They also tool their livestock and the goods that they had acquired in the land of Canaan, and they came into Egypt, Jacob and all his offspring with him, his sons, and his sons' sons with him, his daughters, and his sons' daughters; all his offspring he brought with him into Egypt.

Jacob sent Judah ahead to Joseph to lead the way before him into Goshen. When they came to the land of Goshen Joseph made ready his chariot and went up to meet his father in Goshen. He presented himself to him, fell on his neck and wept on his neck a good while. Jacob said to Joseph, "I can die now, having seen for myself that you are still alive."---Genesis 46: 5-7, 28-30

Finally, father and son embrace, the family is reunited, and a new life has begun for all of them.

The biblical text goes on to narrate how Joseph presented Jacob to Pharaoh, some things Pharaoh told them to do and not to do, things like that. The bible also gives the names of the children of Jacob's sons, children that moved to Egypt. And finally, the bible narrates the death of Jacob, and that Joseph carried his father's body back to Palestine for burial. The narrator follows this up with the story, many years later, of Joseph's own death and how Joseph had made his family promise that, although he would be embalmed, his remains not be buried in Egypt but in the land which the Lord gave to them. This is why, when Moses leads the children of Jacob or Israel (Jacob's other name—see Genesis 32:22-32, esp. vs.28), the texts in Exodus specifically say that they carried the bones of Joseph with them. (Exodus 13:19)

For our purposes this is the conclusion of the story, with Jacob and Joseph reunited and the family together again after so many years. And please, no nonsense about thinking they all lived happily ever after. This is not a fairy tale. It's a long story from the Bible, which is the most realistic book ever compiled. Things were good for Joseph and his brothers for a long while, but then everything turned sour. But that's the story of Moses and the Exodus, another story for another time.

So, with our story coming to its end, meaning that this little book is coming to an end, what have we learned? First: God really does look after or care for His people. Two: God, for His people, brings good out of evil, even in the darkest of times.

After Jacob dies and Joseph buries his father in Palestine, when he returns to Egypt, the text says that his brothers were worried that with Jacob's death, Joseph might be prompted to take his revenge on them. They thought that perhaps Jacob was serving as a block that prevented Joseph from getting back at them, but now, with Jacob gone, there was nothing to prevent Joseph from finally, after all these years, getting back at them for what they did to him.

In chapter fifty, verse twenty Joseph says to his brothers, "You meant evil against me, but God turned it to good, to bring it about that many people should be kept alive as they are today."

You meant evil, but God turned it to good.

That is the theme of this whole story. God brings good out of what people did that was evil. (and, of course, Joseph forgives his brothers and has no intention of taken any sort of revenge on them. See Genesis 50:15-21)

This story, as I have said several times, really and truly points to the cross, which was such an evil act on the part of men, but which God turned into the most amazing, complete and ultimate revelation of his grace and power: the resurrection. In other words, God's turning or transforming the evil that people do into something good, is the very essence of how God works with us, how God works in our lives.

This is a matter of faith. It cannot be proved, as much as we try, to our friends and family. Only if they are predisposed to having faith, even just a little, can they perceive God's hand at work in transforming the evil that has happened in our lives into present good.

What I'm thinking about are the times when, as we move through darkness, it is extremely difficult to see any good in what is happening to us. There's simply no good we can in our lives in such points. Like, when we're in the middle of going through a divorce, and we're alone in our new place with the family gone and it's so quiet, it's hard to see any good coming out of what we're going through.

Or with our job gone and there are, currently, no prospects for employment on the horizon, the bills are now starting to pile up. How are we going to pay them? Or we're laying in our hospital bed after the umpteenth surgery following the accident; we can't return to work, not for a long time, and perhaps not ever. What's going to happen to me, we think. I did nothing. The other car came out of nowhere.

Good come out of this? Seriously?

Or we're sitting at the kitchen table trying desperately to remember just what it is we're accused of doing but which we have absolutely no memory of because once more we were drunk out of our minds. And, if we did what they said we did, an overwhelming sense of shame envelopes us, because we can fully comprehend why our friends and so often members of our own family want nothing to do with us anymore. For God's sake, we don't want anything to do with ourselves anymore! The truth is we'd rather be dead than alive and having to deal with all of this. Good come out of this? Don't make me laugh.

That's what we say.

How can good come out of such evil?

I haven't a clue.

I really don't.

Because the truth is, when we have the guts to admit it, at least in the example I just mentioned, is that we got where we are through our own stupidity, through our own stubbornness, through our own bad choices. And now we have to pay the piper, we have to endure the consequences.

Good emerging through such pain, such estrangement from those we love?

Don't make me laugh.

As in the other examples, though, what we're going through is forced upon us; it's not our fault, at least not entirely. With all these, though, when we get into such a predicament, it's nearly impossible to perceive any good coming out of such an experience.

The truth is there is no way out of such a dark experience save by living through it and enduring what comes our way, and this may take months, perhaps even years.

The hope that can sustain us when we live through such is that the living God, the God of Joseph who saw him through his experience, the God of Jesus, who saw him through his experience and turned that darkness into the glorious light of the resurrection, this same God will give us strength to endure, and will somehow, as only this God can, bring good to us and to others from what we're going through.

This story of Joseph tells how God did this for one man.

By putting this story so early in the biblical narrative, the Holy Spirit reminds us that as God did this to and for Joseph and his family, so God will do for those who trust in him. This is basic to God. We might even say, this way of working with and for his people is part of God's DNA. . . if God had DNA. . . but you perceive what I'm trying to say. This bringing good out of evil is precisely the way God moves and works in the world for and with his people.

The general population at large can never perceive this because this is not so much a matter of fact as it is an assertion emerging from trusting God through one's own dark experiences. It is a matter of faith. This way of trusting God, of being willing to perceive through the eyes of faith, God's working in people's lives to bring good out of the most troubling and difficult experiences, is what the great teachers of the faith have called The Providence of God. God provides and cares for his people in all circumstances, but this can never be proved, only asserted from within the faith community. This Providence is personal, not abstract, not general. It is God caring specifically for God's people in specific ways appropriate to each person, caring for individual men, for specific men, for individual women, for specific women, and for their children, for all those who look to Jesus as the pioneer and perfector of our faith.

One last thing before we end. I got to thinking about that scene with Joseph and his dad, and all his brothers, Reuben, Judah. . . That is a beautiful scene, as they had not seen one another for so many years.

What I got to pondering is that we all, in God's good time, will have a family reunion that will be beyond anything we have experienced in this life, as beautiful as such times have been. All those who have gone on will be there, and we will see them again, our dads, moms, sisters, brothers, cousins, aunts, uncles, friends. . . all those whom we have loved and who have now moved on, and whom we miss so much.

Seeing them, finally, is, I believe, the final place to which the Joseph story points. The reunion of Jacob with his beloved Joseph, the coming together finally of a family that had been estranged from one other for so long, this points to the reunion through Christ that will come eventually to all of us who look to Christ for our final hope. All that has divided us in this life from one another, all that was unhealed at the death of loved ones, all that has divided us, broken us, broken our hearts, by the death of Christ leading into his resurrection, all is forgiven, all is healed and made whole, all is brought back together.

This great truth of the faith is what Jesus himself is

alluding to when he begins his powerful interpretation of his death and resurrection for his disciples on the night before it all happens. In the Gospel of John, chapters 14 – 17 are called The Farewell Discourses, because these chapters form one long lecture by Jesus to his disciples before they go into the Garden of Gethsemane, where, just a few hours later, Jesus is arrested and led away to be crucified. These chapters are Jesus' own interpretation of what his suffering, his going to the cross, mean for his disciples, and for all who look to Jesus for hope and strength. They are some of His most amazing words.

Jesus begins his lecture, as all great teachers do, with a topical sentence leading into a topical paragraph (John 14:1-3) that summarizes succinctly the entire lecture. Here it is: **Let not your hearts be troubled, neither let them be afraid.**

That's the sentence. Carry it with you throughout all of your life, carry it with you into all the circumstances of life. Don't let yourself get over-anxious. And don't be afraid of what might happen to you.

Why?

Because, **"in my Father's house are many dwelling places. If it were not so, would I have told you that I go to prepare a place for you? And if I go and prepare a place for you, I will come again and I will take you to myself, so that where I am, there you may be also."**

That is, everybody's different and special, and everybody goes through the hard parts of life differently. Don't worry. God the Father is with you and will sustain you even to the end and beyond. Because in Jesus, He Himself, has gone through the darkness and transformed it. He will do this for you, He will help your through and will, over time, transform you and your darkness. On top of this, He has a place reserved just for you, and yours. . . .

and Jesus is going through his darkness so that He can go through yours with you and sustain you. That's how he's preparing a place for you. You are not abandoned. You are not left alone. Jesus himself says to us, "I am working to prepare you for your place, and working to reunite you with you and yours so that when the time comes, when your days have come to an end, I will take you home. Home, your real, true home, where your family is waiting for you, and where I am with you and yours forever. "

Talk about a way to end a story!

A PERSONAL NOTE ABOUT BIBLICAL INTERPRETATION, PREACHING AND THE BIBLIOGRAPHY

I need to say something about the bibliography that accompanies this little book. You see, this is not simply a bibliography of the sources I consulted in writing these chapters. It's more than that. It includes works that have shaped how I view human relationships, relationships between men and women, family relationships, friends and on and on. It includes works that are specifically related to human development, works that explore how we grow not just from childhood into adulthood, and works that explore how we grow as spiritual beings.

Many of the works listed are not directly related to the Joseph saga; they are, though, directly related to how I have interpreted this biblical story. As we all know, each one of us brings his or her own experiences and viewpoints when interpreting scripture. This is not to say that our experiences and viewpoints are determinative in our work of interpreting scripture, but they definitely have an effect on our interpretation.

So, because I want to say something about what I have listed in this bibliography, I am also going to have to say some things about how I view biblical interpretation and preaching.

The task of the interpreter, especially a preacher, is to determine as best he or she can, just what the text is saying, first to the preacher him/herself, and then considering what the text said to those who first hear it, and then, thinking about both of these things, coming to perceive what the text is saying to God's people today. This is why the preacher's first task is to read the text, several times, noting what comes before and what comes after. Get this basic story in mind.

Then the preacher is to start checking to see if what he believes to be the message of the text is actually what the text is saying. This sounds more complicated than it is, for all the preacher is trying to do in this second stage is to figure out how this text would have been heard by those for whom it was first written. What would they have understood as being communicated through the text? What was being said to them through these words? In the case of the Joseph story, most biblical scholars believe that, although passed on orally for centuries, the first five books of Moses were probably put in the basic form that we have today sometime after David came to the throne, perhaps during the reign of Solomon. In the case of the New Testament, how would the people in Corinth, or Rome or Ephesus in the last twenty to thirty to forty years in the first century, have understood what is written in the gospels or epistles?

To accomplish this task the preacher must become a biblical scholar, using all the contemporary aids available, including help with the original languages (Hebrew for the Old Testament, Greek for the New), studies in archeology, history, culture, etc. etc. A lot of this is available to the preacher through good, modern, critical commentaries. I think every preacher would agree that these two steps, taken together, form the basic task of correctly interpreting scripture.

Then there is the next step, namely listening for the voice of God speaking through a particular text, to the preacher and to the people to whom the preacher's sermon is directed. This is where interpretation can get interesting. The goal of this third step is achieved when the preacher finally, in the sermon, says to the congregation (or, as well, to the class that the minister is teaching) the Bible says, in this particular text 'A, B and C' and what the preacher says is, in truth, what the biblical text means. That is to say, the preacher's interpretation of the biblical text corresponds directly with how it was heard by those for whom it was originally written and also corresponds to both contemporary and traditional, even ancient, scholarship that deals with the text, and, ultimately, how the text touches the preacher's soul. The preacher with integrity wants her interpretation to so correspond because contrary to what a great many people seem to think, the sermon is not and never has been simply and only the words of the preacher. The sermon is, in a mysterious fashion, also the Word of God to His people today, bringing comfort, bringing hope, bringing peace and challenge. God's Word is most often perceived in a sermon when the sermon is rooted in an informed and faithful analysis of the text (exegesis) that grounds what the preacher says in objective reality. Thus when the preacher begins to say things based on the text, what the preacher says, that is, the preacher's personal interpretation of the text, is not a personal, idiosyncratic interpretation but an interpretation that stands in correspondence with how the text has been interpreted through the centuries.

The preacher's job, therefore, is to be (1) faithful to the original Word as it was heard and (2) faithful to God's people today in helping them hear this word today. Not a different word, but the one word of God in scripture applied to a new situation in a different time among people of a very different culture. For this to happen the preacher must open his own consciousness to this Word. The preacher is the first one to hear God's word speaking to His people today through the text for Sunday's sermon. It is the preacher who is first convicted by the Word. It is the preacher who is first reassured of God's love in Christ as proclaimed by the written Word. It is the preacher who is challenged, sometimes to the depth of her, of his, soul by this written Word.

Only when the written Word speaks powerfully and deeply to the preacher can the preacher then begin to articulate this inner, subjective realization of the Word to God's people more objectively in a sermon. The Word preaches to the preacher, who then preaches this Word, this truth of God, to the congregation.

The preacher is never, EVER, above the congregation, proclaiming some great truth delivered to God's special, preaching servant, set way apart from the congregation. Nor is the preacher beneath the congregation, humble to the point of saying this is the Word of God, but I don't understand it fully, or I don't agree with it and we just have to wrestle with it. Both of these are dodges, ways of avoiding coming to grips with the plain truth of the biblical text.

For true proclamation of the Word of God to occur, the preacher must allow the Word to have its way with him, with her. The preacher must wrestle in his/her own soul with the text, letting the Word of God come into him, into her, deeply, perhaps, sometimes, even painfully. Always this involves the preacher learning humility once again, week after week after week.

If true proclamation is to occur, if the preacher is to preach with integrity, if the Word of God is to penetrate first into the consciousness of the preacher and then is to be proclaimed to the people, then what we perceive the biblical text to be saying will always be shaped by things we have experienced, things we have learned. The basic, original meaning of the biblical text has not changed, but it has become something more, something with more depth and breadth because of the learning and experience we bring to interpreting the bible over time.

This general truth takes a specific form in my interpretation of the Joseph stories. My interpretation has centered on personal development, on family systems, on the development of character, and to a certain extent, on the development of faith itself. This is what I want to acknowledge and, through this bibliography, to share with any who might be interested, many of the works that have contributed to my perceiving these biblical texts in this manner.

I also realize that, to a lot of people, any sort of biblical interpretation that comes across as psychological in any way is, in some sense, suspect.

To which I say: you can't please everyone.

I'm certainly not about to say that my interpretation is the right one, or the only one. I'm a protestant, for goodness' sake, and firmly believe that the bible can be faithfully interpreted by anyone, so long as they submit themselves to the guidance of the Holy Spirit and are dutifully humble in their interpretation. And, with some caveats, giving due recognition to interpretations in the past. After all, the Bible has been around a long time, and Christianity has had so many great teachers. It's downright silly to think our personal interpretation of a biblical text is unique and outstanding. The only reason a preacher might think this stems from the fact that he or she is simply too lazy to do good research.

I admit that I usually go beyond simply repeating what the biblical text said. It's not our job as preachers with integrity to simply parrot the text. The text must not just be explicated but applied.

Throughout the previous chapters I have drawn some conclusions from the biblical text which the text did not specifically state. This is particularly true when dealing with the characters' feelings and motivations, something which we moderns are desperately interested in but which the biblical text is most usually quite reticent about. I do not believe I am out of line in these suppositions, but obviously some may disagree. That's fine. It's still a free country.

However, in no instance do I believe I have falsified what the biblical text was teaching. In everything I have said I firmly believe that I have not only stayed close to the biblical text, but I believe I have honestly come to grips with the basic truth the text is communicating for God's people, and I have drawn this truth out in such a way so as to make it credible, perhaps even challenging for the people of God in the twenty-first century in the United States of America.

Now, every preacher I know and most of those I don't know would be willing to affirm what I have just written, applying it to their own teaching and sermons. Nothing special there. But the bottom line here is that I know there are a lot of works in this bibliography that have, at first glance, nearly nothing to do with the bible, the Old Testament, the church or anything related to such things. And if they don't, then some are bound to ask: what do such works have to do with biblical interpretation?

It all has to do with what shapes one's own self, one's own consciousness. This affects how we perceive what the biblical text is saying. My consciousness has been shaped profoundly by every work listed in this bibliography, particularly in my interpretation of the Joseph stories. Every work listed is crucially important in shaping how I heard God speaking to me and then to His people through these stories about Joseph the dreamer. You may not perceive the connection but, trust me, it's there.

That's why such works are listed in this bibliography. I hope your interest may be piqued, enough so that you check out some of these non-biblical books. You just might be surprised at what you read, surprised in a good way. At least, I hope so.

BIBLIOGRAPHY

Bibles

Biblia Hebraica Stuttgartensia Standard Edition, German Bile Society, 1977

Novum Testamentum Graece, (critical apparatus prepared by Erwin Nestle and Kurt Aland), Privileg.Wurtt, Bibelanstalt Stuttgart, Germany, 1960

Synopsis Quattuor Evangeliorum, Editio Octava, prepared & edited by Aland, Kurt, Wuerttembergische Bibelanstalt Stuttgart, copyright 1967, 1973 Edition

The Interlinear Hebrew-Aramaic OLD TESTAMENT, Volume I, Second Edition, Green, Jay P., Sr., General Editor and Translator, Hendrickson Publishers, Peabody, MA, 1985

The Interlinear Greek-English NEW TESTAMENT, Second Edition, Green, Jay P. Sr., General Editor and Translator, Hendrickson Publishers, Peabody, MA 1985

The Holy Bible, authorized King James Version, The National Bible Press, Philadelphia, PA, printed 1944 (Personal note: this was my Grandmother Young's large print version)

The Oxford Annotated Bible, Revised Standard Version, Oxford University Press, London and New York, 1962

The Holy Bible, New Revised Standard Version, copyright 1989 by the Division of Christian Education of the National Council of the Churches of Christ in the United States of America, published by Zondervan Publishing House, Grand Rapids, Michigan

The Jerusalem Bible, Reader's Edition, Doubleday & Company, Inc.,

Garden City, New York, 1968

The New English Bible, with the Apocrypha, Oxford University Press and Cambridge University Press, 1970

Disciples Study Bible, New International Version, Holman bible Publishers, Nashville, TN, 1988

Today's English Version (aka *The Good News Bible*), The American Bible Society, New York, NY, 1992

General

Achtemeier, Elizabeth, *Creative Preaching Finding the Words,* Abingdon Press, Nashville, TN, 1980

--------------------------- , *Nature, God and Pulpit,* William B. Eerdmans Publishing Company, Grand Rapids, Michigan, 1992

---------------------------, *The Old Testament and the Proclamation of the Gospel,* The Westminster Press, Philadelphia, PA, 1973

---------------------------, *Preaching As Theology & Art,* Abingdon Press, Nashville, TN, 1984

---------------------------, *Preaching from the Old Testament,* Westminster/ John Knox Press, Louisville, KY 1989

---------------------------, *Preaching Hard Texts of the Old Testament,* Hendrickson Publishers, Inc., Peabody, MA, 1998

Barth, Karl, *Church Dogmatics I/I, The Doctrine of the Word of God, Prolegomena to Church Dogmatics,* T. & T. Clark, Ltd, Edinburgh, 1936

-------------- *Church Dogmatics, I/II, The Doctrine of the Word of God, Prolegomena to Church Dogmatics, Second Half,* T. & T. Clark, Ltd, Edinburgh, 1956

-------------*Church Dogmatics, II/I, The Doctrine of God, First Half,* T. & T. Clark, Ltd, Edinburgh, 1957

-------------*Church Dogmatics, II/II, The Doctrine of God, Second Half,* T. & T. Clark, Ltd, Edinburgh, 1957

-------------*Church Dogmatics, III/III, The Doctrine of Creation,* T & T Clark, Edinburgh, 1960 (Particularly Section 48 "The Doctrine of Providence, Its Basis and Form" and Section 49 "God the Father as Lord of His Creature, pgs. 3-288)

-------------*The Word of God and the Word of Man*, translated by Douglas Horton, Harper & Brothers, New York, 1957

Berkhof, Louis, *Reformed Dogmatics, Second Revised and Enlarged Edition*, Wm. B. Eerdmans Publishing Co, Grand Rapids, Michigan, 1941

Bonhoeffer, Dietrich, *The Cost of Discipleship, Second Edition*, The Macmillan Company, New York, 1959

------------------------- *Creation and Fall, Temptation Two Biblical Studies*, Macmillan Publishing Co., Inc., New York, 1959

Bowen, Murray, *Family Therapy in Clinical Practice*, Rowman & Littlefield Publishers Ltd.,2004

Bright, John, *A History of Israel, Second Edition*, The Westminster Press, Philadelphia, PA 1972

Brueggemann, Walter, *Genesis*, in the commentary series *Interpretation: A Bible Commentary for Teaching and Preaching*, John Knox Press, Atlanta, GA 1982

Calvin, John, *Institutes of the Christian Religion*, ed. John T. McNeill, trans. Ford Lewis Battles, The Westminster Press, Philadelphia, 1960

Childs, Brevard S., *Introduction to the Old Testament as Scripture*, Fortress Press, Philadelphia, PA 1979

---------------------- *Old Testament Theology in a Canonical Context*, Fortress Press, Philadelphia, PA 1985

Clift, Jean Dalby and Clift, Wallace B., *Symbols of Transformation in Dreams*, Crossroad Publishing Company, New York, NY, 1984

Dent, Barbara, *My Only Friend is Darkness--Living the Night of Faith with St. John of the Cross*, ICS Publications, Institute of Carmelite Studies, Washington, D.C., 1992, originally published by Ave Maria Press, Notre Dame, Indiana, 1988

Edwards, Lloyd, *How We Belong, Fight and Pray The MBTI as a Key to Congregational Dynamics*, The Alban Institute Inc, 1993

Egan, Harvey D., *What Are They Saying About Mysticism?*, Paulist Press,

New York, NY and Ramsey, NJ., 1982

Erikson, Erik H., *Childhood and Society,* W. W. Norton, New York, NY, 1951, revised edition 1963

--------------------, *Identity: Youth and Crisis,* Faber and Faber, New York, NY 1971

Fowler, James W., *Becoming Adult, Becoming Christian--Adult Development and Christian Faith,* Harper & Row Publishers, San Francisco, CA 1984

Friedman, Edwin H., *Generation to Generation--Family Process in Church and Synagogue,* The Guilford Press, 1985

Gilbert, Roberta M., *The Eight Concepts of Bowen Theory--A New Way of Thinking About The Individual and The Group,* Leading Systems Press, Fall Church & Basye, VA 2006

Groeschel, Benedict J., *Spiritual Passages-- The Psychology of Spiritual Development,* Crossroad Publishing Co., New York, NY 1988

---------------------------- *Understanding Spiritual Development,* Credence Cassettes, The National Catholic Reporter Publishing Co., Kansas City, MO 1988

Hall, Calvin S. and Nordby, Vernon J., *A Primer of Jungian Psychology,* the New American Library, Inc., New York, NY 1973

Hall, James A., *Jungian Dream Interpretation-- A Handbook of Theory and Practice,* Inner City Books, Toronto, Canada, 1983

Hancock, Angela Dienhart, *Karl Barth's Emergency Homiletic 1932-1933 A Summons to Prophetic Witness at the Dawn of the Third Reich,* Wm B. Eerdmans Publishing Co., Grand Rapids, Michigan, 2013

Hands, Donald R. and Fehr, Wayne L., *Spiritual Wholeness for Clergy-- A New Psychology of Intimacy with God, Self and Others,* The Alban Institute Press, 1993

Holmes, Urban T., *A History of Christian Spirituality--An Analytical Introduction,* Morehouse Publishing, Harrisburg, PA 2002 (Note: originally published by The Seabury Press, New York, NY, 1980)

Jacobi, Jolande, *The Psychology of C. G. Jung, Eighth Edition,* Yale University Press, 1973

St. John of the Cross, *The Collected Works of St. John of the Cross*, trans. Kieran Kavanaugh, Otilio Rodriguez, ICS Publications, Institute of Carmelite Studies, Washington D. C., 1973

Johnson, Robert A., *He Understanding Masculine Psychology*, Harper & Row Publishers, 1974

----------------------, *Owning Your Own Shadow Understanding the Dark Side of the Psyche*, Harper SanFrancisco, 1991

----------------------, *She Understanding Feminine Psychology*, Harper & Row Publishers, 1976

Jung, C. G., *Dreams*, trans. by R. F. C. Hull, MJF Books, New York, NY, copyright Princeton University Press, 1974

Kelsey, Morton T., *Caring--How Can We Love One Another?*, Paulist Press, Ramsey, NJ, 1981

--------------------, *Dreams--A Way to Listen to God*, Paulist Press, New York, NY and Ramsey, NJ, 1978

--------------------, *Encounter with God--A Theology of Christian Experience*, Paulist Press, Mahwah, NJ, 1972

--------------------, *Prophetic Ministry--The Psychology and Spirituality of Pastoral Care*, The Crossroad Publishing Company, New York, NY, 1982

--------------------, *Resurrection--Release From Oppression*, Paulist Press, Mahwah, NJ, 1985

Keirsey, David and Bates, Marilyn, *Please Understand Me Character & Temperament Types*, Fifth Edition, Gnosology Books Ltd, 1984

Kempis, Thomas A, *The Imitation of Christ*, translated by Leo Sherley-Price, Penguine Books Ltd, Harmondsworth & Middlesex, England, 1952

Kierkegaard, Soren, *Fear and Trembling and the Sickness Unto Death*, trans by Walter Lowrie, Princeton University Press, Princeton, New Jersey, 1954

Langley, Raymond J., *The Writings of C. G. Jung*, Monarch Press, New York, NY 1970

Leith, John H., *Basic Christian Doctrine*, Westminster/John Knox Press,

Louisville, KY 1993

------------------ *From Generation to Generation The Renewal of the Church According to Its Own Theology and Practice*, Westminster/John Knox Press, Louisville, 1990

------------------*The Reformed Imperative What the Church Has to Say That No One Else Can Say,* The Westminster Press, Philadelphia, PA, 1988

May, Gerald G., *The Dark Night of the Soul--A Psychiatrist Explores the Connection Between Darkness and Spiritual Growth,* HarperCollins Publishers, New York, NY, 2004

McCormack, Bruce L., *Karl Barth's Critically Realistic Dialectical Theology Its Genesis and Development 1900-1936,* Oxford University Press, 1997

Merton, Thomas, *Contemplative Prayer,* Doubleday & Company, Garden City, NY, 1969

-------------------, *New Seeds of Contemplation,* New Directions Publishing Corporation, New York, NY, 1961

-------------------, *Thoughts in Solitude Reflections on the Spiritual Life and the Love of Solitude,* Doubleday and Company, Garden City, New York, 1958

Michael, Chester P. and Norrisey, Marie C., *Prayer and Temperament Different Prayer Forms for Different Personality Types,* The Open Door Inc., Charlottesville, VA 1984

Myers, Isabel Briggs and McCaulley, Mary H., *Manual: A Guide to the Development and Use of the Myers-Briggs Type Indicator, Second Edition,* Consulting Psychologists Press, Palo Alto, CA, 1985

Myers, Isabel Briggs, revised by Kirby, Linda and Myers, Katherine D., *Introduction to Type--A guide to Understanding Your Results on the Myers-Briggs Type Indicator, Sixth Edition,* Consulting Psychologists Press, Inc., Palo Alto, CA, 1998

Niebuhr, H. Richard, *Faith on Earth, An Inquiry into the Structure of Human Faith,* Yale University Press, New Haven & London, 1989

------------------------, *The Meaning of Revelation,* Macmillan Publishing Co, Ltd, New York, NY, 1941

----------------------, *Radical Monotheism and Western Culture with Supplementary Essays*, Harper & Row Publishers, 1960

----------------------, *The Responsible Self An Essay in Christian Moral Philosophy*, Harper & Row Publishers, 1963

Oswald, Roy M. and Kroeger, Otto, *Personality Type and Religious Leadership*, The Alban Institute Press, Inc., Washington, D. C., 1988

Pearman, Roger R. and Albritton, Sarah C., *I'm Not Crazy, I'm Just Not You--The Real Meaning of the 16 Personality Types*, Davis-Black Publishing, Palo Alto, CA, 1997

Quenk, Naomi L., *In the Grip--Understanding Type, Stress and the Inferior Function, Second Edition*, Consulting Psychologists Press, Inc., Mountain View, CA, 2000

Pennington, M. Basil, *Daily We Touch Him   Practical Religious Experiences*, Doubleday & Co. Inc, Garden City, New York, 1977

von Rad, Gerhard, *Genesis, Revised Edition*, in the commentary series The Old Testament Library, The Westminster Press, Philadelphia, PA, 1974

---------------------- *Old Testament Theology, Vol. I and II*, Harper & Row, New York, NY, 1963 and 1965

Riso, Don Richard, with Hudson, Russ, *Personality Types Using the Enneagram for Self-Discovery, Revised Edition*, Houghton Mifflin Company, Boston, MA and New York, NY, 1996

---, *The Wisdom of the Enneagram The Complete Guide to Psychological and Spiritual Growth for the Nine Personality Types*, Bantam Books, New York, NY, 1999

Sanford, John A., *Between People: Communicating One-to-One*, Paulist Press, New York, NY/Ramsey, NJ 1982

----------------------*Dreams--God's Forgotten Language*, J. P. Lippincott Company, New York, NY, 1968

----------------------*Evil The Shadow Side of Reality*, Crossroad Publishing Co, New York, 1989

---- ---------------- *The Man Who Wrestled With God--Light from the Old

Testament on the Psychology of Individuation, Paulist Press, Ramsey, NJ, 1981

--------------------*The Strange Trial of Mr. Hyde A New Look at the Nature of Human Evil*, Harper & Row, San Franscisco, 1987

------------------- and Lough, George, *What Men are Like--The Psychology of Men, for Men and the Women Who Live with Them*, Paulist Press, Mahweh, NJ, 1988

Sheridan, Mark, ed., *Genesis 12-50, Ancient Christian Commentary on Scripture, Old Testament, Vol. II,* Intervarsity Press, Downers Grove, IL, 2002

Singer, June, *Boundaries of the Soul The Practice of Jung's Psychology, Revised and Updated,* Bantam Doubleday Dell Publishing Group, Inc., New York, NY, 1994

Swindoll, Charles R., *Joseph: From Pit to Pinnacle, A Bible Study Guide,* Insight for Living, Fullerton, CA 1979

Toman, Walter, *Family Constellation Its Effects on Personality and Social Behavior, Fourth Edition,* Springer Publishing Co, NY, 1993

Tupper, E. Frank, *A Scandalous Providence--The Jesus Story of the Compassion of God,* Mercer University Press, Macon, GA, 1995

Underhill, Evelyn, *The Fruits of the Spirit, Light of Christ, Abba,* David McKay Company, Inc., New York, NY, 1956

--------------------, *The Spiritual Life,* Mowbray, London & Oxford, 1955

Welch, John, *When Gods Die--An Introduction to John of the Cross,* Paulist Press, Mahwah, NJ, 1990

Westermann, Claus, *Handbook to the Old Testament,* trans. by Robert H. Boyd, Augsburg Publishing House, Minneapolis, MN, 1967

White, Victor, *God and the Unconscious,* Spring Publications, Dallas, TX, 1982 first published in Great Britain in 1952

Whitehead, Evelyn Eaton and Whitehead, James D., *Christian Life Patterns--The Psychological Challenges and Religious Invitations of Adult Life,* Doubleday & Company, Inc., Garden City, New York, NY, 1979, reissued 1982

ABOUT THE AUTHOR

James R. M. Young

James Young has served as a parish minister in the Presbyterian Church (USA) for over forty-one years. He holds a Bachelor's degree in History from Davidson College (Davidson, NC), a Master's in Education from The Presbyterian School of Christian Education (in Richmond, VA). and the Doctor of Ministry degree from Union Theological Seminary (Richmond, VA) In 1998 he was named to National Directory's Who's Who in Executives and Professionals. Though now retired, he continues to study theology and the bible, along with occasionally preaching and speaking in churches and other venues. He has four grown daughters and lives in the southern region of the Shenandoah Valley in Virginia.